D0325710

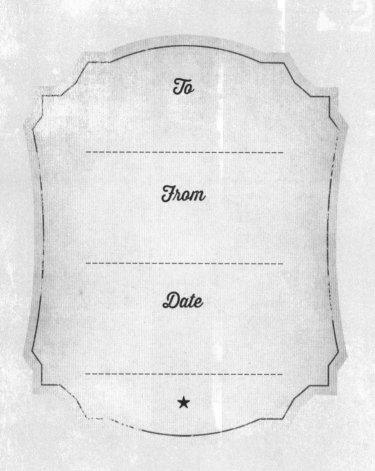

To

From

Date

★

001171

Sunshine

FOR THE SOUL

MORNING
DEVOTIONS
*to warm the
heart*

DaySpring

LIVE YOUR FAITH

Sunshine for the Soul: Morning Devotions to Warm the Heart
© 2019 DaySpring Cards, Inc. All rights reserved.
First Edition, December 2019

Published by:

P.O. Box 1010
Siloam Springs, AR 72761
dayspring.com

All rights reserved. Sun*shine for the Soul: Morning Devotions to Warm the Heart* is under copyright protection. No part of this book may be used or reproduced in any manner whatsoever without written permission except in the case of brief quotations embodied in critical articles and reviews.

Scriptures quotations marked NIV are taken from the Holy Bible, New International Version®, NIV®. Copyright © 1973, 1978, 1984, 2011 by Biblica, Inc.® Used by permission of Zondervan. All rights reserved worldwide. www.zondervan.com. The "NIV" and "New International Version" are trademarks registered in the United States Patent and Trademark Office by Biblica, Inc.®

Scripture quotations marked GW are taken from GOD'S WORD®, © 1995 God's Word to the Nations. Used by permission of God's Word Mission Society.

Scripture quotations marked GNT are taken from the Good News Translation in Today's English Version- Second Edition Copyright © 1992 by American Bible Society. Used by Permission.

Scripture quotations marked NKJV are taken from the New King James Version. Copyright © 1982 by Thomas Nelson, Inc. Used by permission. All rights reserved.

Scripture quotations marked KJV are taken from the Holy Bible, King James Version.

Scripture quotations marked NLT are taken from the Holy Bible, New Living Translation, copyright © 1996, 2004, 2007 by Tyndale House Foundation. Used by permission of Tyndale House Publishers, Inc., Carol Stream, Illinois 60188. All rights reserved.

Scripture quotations marked ESV are taken from the ESV Bible® (The Holy Bible, English Standard Version®) copyright ©2001 by Crossway Bibles, a publishing ministry of Good News Publishers. Used by permission. All rights reserved.

Scripture quotations marked THE MESSAGE are taken from THE MESSAGE, copyright © 1993, 1994, 1995, 1996, 2000, 2001, 2002 by Eugene H. Peterson. Used by permission of NavPress. All rights reserved. Represented by Tyndale House Publishers, Inc.

Scripture quotations marked BEREAN are taken from The Holy Bible, Berean Study Bible, BSB Copyright ©2016, 2018 by Bible Hub. Used by Permission. All Rights Reserved Worldwide.

Scripture quotations marked NASB are taken from the NEW AMERICAN STANDARD BIBLE®, Copyright © 1960, 1962, 1963, 1968, 1971, 1972, 1973, 1975, 1977, 1995 by The Lockman Foundation. Used by permission.

Scripture quotations marked AMP are taken from the Amplified Bible, Copyright © 2015 by The Lockman Foundation. Used by permission.

Written by: Linda Kozar
Cover Design: Brian Bobel
Printed in China
Prime: J1597
ISBN: 978-1-64454-446-4

CONTENTS

PORCH SITTING

Love your neighbor as yourself.
GALATIANS 5:14 NIV

Southern porches are perfect for sunny, sultry weather. There's usually a cushioned swing with a faded old quilt, a collection of white wicker chairs, a rocking chair or two, and big oversized ferns hanging from the porch ceiling. Porch ferns cannot be too big. That's a fact. And if you have a heavenly-scented honeysuckle or jasmine plant twined on the pillars, life is good indeed. The only thing you can add to a perfect day of porch sitting is a big pitcher of homemade lemonade and a plate of homemade sugar cookies. Whether you have company beside you or are all by your lonesome, you know you're gonna have a grand old time on your swing, or rocker, or flapping your jaw. Drawn like bees to the scent of sugar, neighbors are sure to stop by for cookies and conversation. Some of them even go a-porching down the street, stopping at every porch and veranda to nibble up tasty treats and tidbits of news. Neighborhood dogs sometimes race up the porch steps for some love and maybe a dog biscuit or two from a handy jar.

We need each other in this world. God put you next to your neighbors for a reason, to pray for and with them, to help one another, and perhaps to hold power tools ransom for another plate of homemade sugar cookies.

FAITH CHECK

Most of all, though, sitting on a porch is relaxing. Maybe God had a porch in mind when He created a day of rest for us. Life only simmers down when we let it. We all need a leisurely day to listen to bees buzzing around, to watch children play hopscotch, and admire the camellias.

Rest is the ability to
totally trust God without
living under the stress
of the cares of life.

—PERRY STONE

★

THERE IS A TIME

*Who knows if perhaps you were made queen
for just such a time as this?*
ESTHER 4:14 NLT

sther realized that God had placed her in a unique position as queen of a foreign nation. She decided to risk her life in order to save her people. During the American Revolution, Lydia Darragh faced a similar decision. In September of 1777, British troops under General William Howe had occupied her town and her residence. She and her family were allowed to remain in their home only because they were Quakers who were known to be pacifists. However, Lydia was not only a Quaker, she was a mother, whose oldest son, Charles, had enlisted in the Second Pennsylvania Regiment of the Continental Army. So, she began to eavesdrop on Howe's staff meetings held in her own parlor, and discovered they were planning a surprise attack. Lydia wrote down the vital information in code and, under the pretense of filling her flour bag at the grist mill, made her way to George Washington's camp to warn the Continental Army, thus saving the men from annihilation by the British troops.

FAITH CHECK

One day you, too, might be in a pivotal position, one that God Himself has placed you in, and you may have a difficult decision to make, a decision that might cost you everything. "Those who love their life in this world will lose it. Those who care nothing for their life in this world will keep it for eternity" (John 12:25 NLT).

In God's hands, intended
evil becomes eventual good.

–MAX LUCADO

PILLARS OF SOCIETY

The earth and all who dwell in it melt;
it is I who have firmly set its pillars.

PSALM 75:3 NASB

illars of society are people who are generally thought of as tireless volunteers and givers, people who are influential at championing worthy causes. But in the ancient world if you wanted future generations to remember your name, you built a pillar. King David's son Absalom wanted to be remembered for something in life besides his luxurious hair. So he erected a pillar honoring himself in the King's Valley and called it "Absalom's Monument" (II Samuel 18:18 NIV). But not all pillars in this world are alike. Did you know that monuments can also be condiments? Lot and his family left Sodom at dawn. God's angels had warned them not to look back. However, once Lot, his daughters, and his wife were safely near the town of Zoar, the destruction began. Fire and brimstone exploded into the sky and rained down death and destruction. Everyone they knew and everything they owned was gone in a flash. Sadly, Lot's wife resisted looking back like Eve resisted the fruit (Genesis 19:26) and turned into a pillar of salt. And so it is that Lot's wife forever looks back in her salty way to the sinful life that once captivated her.

FAITH CHECK

It is far better to be an eternal pillar in God's kingdom. A pillar set on a firm foundation helps to support the whole structure and keeps it standing. God says, "He who overcomes, I will make him a pillar in the temple of My God" (Revelation 3:12 NASB).

What were Lot's last
words to his wife?
"Is someone following us?"

★

FACTS ABOUT
ABSALOM

*Absalom, King David's son, was a handsome man.
In fact, it was said that there was not another
man in all of David's kingdom that was as good
looking as Absalom. There was not a flaw in him
from head to toe and besides that, he had
a head of ridiculously thick, gorgeous
and ultra-luxurious hair.*

SEVEN FACTS ABOUT ABSALOM'S HAIR:

1. Absalom only cut his hair once a year and the hair he cut off weighed five pounds (2 Samuel 14:26 ESV).

2. His hair was likely thirty times thicker than normal human hair.

3. In ancient times there was no shampoo. Some people used oil mixed with natron, a mineral deposit similar to baking soda to wash their bodies and perhaps their hair.

4. Absalom anointed his hair daily with fragrant perfumed oils and ointments.

5. He sprinkled gold dust on his hair in the fashion of the men of court so that the bright sun would reflect and shimmer off the gold.

6. Might have worn his hair wound up on top of his head like a crown and fastened it with ivory pins.

7. His hair was so dense and thick and strong that when it got tangled in a tree branch, his donkey kept right on going and Absalom was left dangling by his hair on the branch, a vulnerable target for Joab, who took Absalom's life (2 Samuel 18:14).

SOURCE:

https://www.studylight.org/commentary/2-samuel/14-26.html (Joseph Benson's Commentary of the Old and New Testaments)

https://womenfromthebook.com/tag/ancient-shampoo/

FROM FOWL TO FOREVER

His banner over me was love.
SONG OF SOLOMON 2:4 ESV

Male bowerbirds, native to Australia and Papua New Guinea, go "all out" to attract a mate. They build elaborately arched constructions called "bowers" out of parallel sticks, moss, red berries, saliva, and chewed-up vegetable matter. Romantic. The clever birds use their beaks to place the sticks so that they arch inward to form a cozy love nest. They scrounge around for flowers, colorful bits and pieces of shells, plastics, and shiny objects to make their bower stand out to choosy females. The fanciest ones receive the most attention from the female birds, but the deciding factor on choosing the right mate is not based purely on architecture. Females expect the male to entertain them with an intricate dance involving chirps, whistles, and buzzing sounds. And after all that effort, if a male bowerbird is chosen by a female, he does not mate with her for life. Go figure.

FAITH CHECK

Singles of the human kind often feel frustrated at the process of finding a spouse as well. Like the bowerbirds, we have our worldly checklists as to what we want in a husband or wife. We build our own versions of bowers, composed of flowers and shiny new cars and expensive gifts, but those things and all the fancy footwork on the dance floor can only entertain, not sustain a true relationship. Look for the fruit of the Spirit in a potential spouse: love, joy, peace, forbearance, kindness, goodness, faithfulness, gentleness and self-control (Galatians 5:22–23). We all belong under the banner of His love, not under a bower of worldly desires.

I want someone who will
look at me the same way
I look at chocolate cake.

★

THUNDERS AND WHISPERS

Call to Me, and I will answer you, and show you great and mighty things, which you do not know.
JEREMIAH 33:3 NKJV

A lull in the conversation between strangers or acquaintances is often uncomfortable, while conversations with loved ones and close friends are sprinkled with familiar pauses and breaks. But what happens when God is silent and that silence is more than a pause or a lull? As close as King David felt to the Lord, he wondered at times if God had forsaken him. "O my God, I cry by day, but you do not answer, and by night, but I find no rest" (Psalm 22:2 ESV). There are times in our prayer life and in our earnest conversations with God that He goes unusually silent. Is He distracted or uninterested in hearing us pour our hearts out to Him? Could He be bored? Quite the opposite. The Psalmist in 55:16–17 (NIV) says, "As for me, I call to God...and He hears my voice." God is listening. He's just not answering in the way you expect Him to.

FAITH CHECK

God speaks in both thunders and whispers, but in His silence He speaks much more. Silence is a time for self-reflection, for listening. Lean into the silence. Be still with Him. Ask God to show you if there is a sin you need to come clean about. Is it truly possible for God to be silent if your Bible is right there next to you? If you want to talk to someone, you pick up your phone to call or text. If you want to hear from God, open His Word, the Bible. When you call unto Him, God promises to show you great and mighty things. Our hearts hear God better than our ears.

The words "listen" and "silent" have the same letters of the alphabet.

★

THE ABUNDANCE OF LITTLE

Many are called, but few are chosen.
MATTHEW 22:14 ESV

When we want something, we tend to think of bigger as better. More rather than less. We want a bigger house. Lots of money. Larger portions of food. We want our lives to overflow with an overabundance of everything. Israel was impressed with Saul because he was a tall drink of water. But God looks at the heart, and King Saul's heart was not right before God. In God's economy, little is much. He can take a shepherd boy and transform him into King David (I Samuel 16:13). He can save a widow and her family from starvation with an ever-flowing cruet of oil (II Kings 4:2). Jesus can take a little boy's lunch of a few loaves and fishes and feed thousands with leftovers to spare (John 6:1–14). God can raise up a farmer like Gideon (Judges 7:1–7) to lead a ragtag army of a few hundred men against thousands of soldiers and prevail against them. "Five of you will chase a hundred, and a hundred of you will chase ten thousand, and your enemies will fall by the sword before you" (Leviticus 26:8 NIV). Over and over in Scripture, God chooses the lowly, the underdog, the youngest and most inexperienced, and the least likely to succeed based on human assessment. And inexplicably, from the least of us, He brings forth much.

FAITH CHECK

As the old hymn goes, "Little is much when God is in it! Labor not for wealth or fame; there's a crown, and you can win it, if you go in Jesus's name." —Kittie Louise Suffield

God chooses the unlikely
to do the unimaginable.

★

THE HOMECOMING

This my son was dead, and is alive again;
he was lost, and is found. And they began to celebrate.
LUKE 15:24 ESV

Most of us know the story of the prodigal son. He got the bright idea of asking his father to give him his inheritance early so he could journey to a far country and party hearty. But the gravity of the request escaped him. Asking for an early inheritance was an extreme insult, like telling his dad he wished he were dead. Though his heart was wounded to the core, the father gave his son what he asked. And the son pursued a path of reckless living until he was so poor he couldn't jump over a nickel to save a dime. He was so hungry the carob pods he was feeding the pigs started to look good. So he decided to return home even if he had to work as a servant in his father's house. Meanwhile, back at the ranch, his loving father kept praying for him to return home. And when he spotted the tiny speck of his son in the distance, he ran to embrace him. He was so overjoyed to have his son back, he called for the servants to bring the best robe for his son to wear, to put shoes on his feet and a ring on his hand, and to prepare a feast to celebrate his son's return.

FAITH CHECK

The prodigal's father is a wonderful example of how our loving Father receives us when we repent and "come home." Can we do less with people who have wounded or disappointed us? The prodigal's hard-working obedient brother wasn't feeling the sunshine and lollipops, but his father reassured him of his good standing. What the older brother failed to appreciate was the return of his younger sibling from the death of sin to eternal life. Salvation is truly cause for celebration.

God's mercy is bigger than any mistake you've made.

★

THE GRAVITY OF SIN

Watch and pray, lest you fall into temptation.
The spirit indeed is willing, but the flesh is weak.
MATTHEW 26:41 NKJV

merican clergyman and evangelist Billy Sunday once said, "Temptation is the devil looking through the keyhole. Yielding is opening the door and inviting him in." The pull of temptation can feel as strong as the gravitational pull of the earth, drawing us to worldly pursuits that will only drag us downward into the muck and mire of sin. But those who are of the Spirit are to be heavenly minded, not earthly minded. Though we cannot escape the physics of gravity on this earth, we can overcome the gravity of temptation. Jesus showed us how. "We do not have a high priest who is unable to sympathize with our weaknesses, but one who in every respect has been tempted as we are, yet without sin" (Hebrews 4:15 ESV). God doesn't tempt us but He does allow us to be tempted so that we can learn to overcome those temptations and become stronger in His strength (I John 2:14).

FAITH CHECK

At the Last Supper, Jesus washed the feet of the disciples, perhaps because their feet were the point of contact to the earth. Our earthly bodies are tethered for now to the earth from which we were created, but those who are born again are new creations in Christ. Though our feet touch the earth, the rest of our bodies point toward heaven. Those who are heavenly minded turn their hearts and thoughts to a greater connection, the promise of eternal life far from sin's tether.

Opportunity may knock
only once, but temptation
leans on the doorbell.

★

9
GOOD ADVICE

For the LORD gives wisdom;
from His mouth come knowledge and understanding.
PROVERBS 2:6 NIV

Don't you wish your grown kids would listen to your advice? Their lives would be so much easier if they would just hear what you have to say. After all, you *learned* the hard way, by experience. And you *earned* the hard-won knowledge you now want to *pass* on to them. However, all your kids want to do is pass on your advice. American author and motivational speaker Leo Buscaglia once said, "Those who think they know it all have no way of finding out they don't." Why's that? Because know-it-alls aren't interested in pursuing truth or knowledge. They already know all they want to know. If only it were as easy to take advice as to give it. Young people don't have the market cornered on haughtiness though. The truth is, we are all a bit hardheaded. Ask God how He knows! He speaks to us through His Word, the Bible. He communicates to our hearts. Yet we often ignore Him and do as we please instead. How frustrating must it be for God to see us get hurt time and time again because we chose not to listen to Him!

FAITH CHECK

When you look back on your own life, remember and appreciate the wise advice your own parents tried to give you, advice you chose to ignore. They say that time gives valuable advice. But God's wisdom is priceless.

Look back and thank
God. Look forward and
trust God. But most of
all, just plain trust Him.

★

10
TASTY TIDBITS

A good name is more desirable than great riches.
PROVERBS 22:1 NIV

ave you ever suffered the slings and arrows of vicious gossip? As rumors and gossip spread, the narrative gets bigger and juicier while your name and reputation shrink daily to new lows. To those who spread gossip, their idle words are just words. To the object of such abusive behavior, those words are weapons that wound with every parting of the lips. The emotional pain can be overwhelming. Whether rumors spark from a chance conversation or a deliberately crafted lie, the devastation is the same. Sadly, many of those who eagerly share tasty tidbits about you are people you consider to be your friends. Friendship is a broad definition, however. True friends are people you would trust your life with. Friends can be family members, neighbors, coworkers, church friends, and acquaintances of every sort. There are friends on social media as well. Are all of these people your friends? As the saying goes, there are friends, and there are friends.

FAITH CHECK

A true friend will uphold your character before others and will stand by your side when no one else will. Today you may be the object of gossip, but tomorrow you may be one of the talebearers, the cause of great personal pain to someone else. Remember, rumors don't become rumors if you choose not to repeat them. Once spoken, words can be forgiven, but never forgotten.

People will always
question all the good
things they hear about
you but believe all the bad
without a second thought.

THE SLIPPERY SLOPE

Who has held the dust of the earth in a basket,
or weighed the mountains on the scales
and the hills in a balance?
ISAIAH 40:12 NIV

This verse offers a mental picture of God the Father. How do *you* see God? Is He some sort of gargantuan Paul Bunyan figure who can pick up mountains and weigh them on a scale? Or is He an ethereal being sitting on a faraway throne? The prophet Isaiah sought to remind the backslidden Israelites about the greatness and majesty of God. So Isaiah lists feats that can only be accomplished by Almighty God, definitely not by pagan idols crafted of wood or metal. But instead of heeding the prophet's plea, the people continued to worship graven images with stubborn zeal. The idols in front of them seemed more logical to them than the invisible God of their fathers. So they settled for idols created by their own hands rather than the Creator of all things.

Whatever your concept of God, or how you picture Him in your imagination, your imagination will fall far short when your eyes behold His glory. "Blessed are they that have not seen, and yet have believed" (John 20:29 KJV).

FAITH CHECK

Many of us are as foolish today as the Israelites of yesterday. An idol doesn't have to look like an idol to be one. We can put our relationships or jobs before God. Worship a house, car, boat, bank account, or just about anything before Him. God knows what stubborn looks like. He never gave up on the Israelites and He will never give up on you.

The best way to avoid going downhill is to stay off the slope.

—WOODROW KROLL

★

SAILING STONES

You yourselves like living stones are being built up as a
spiritual house, to be a holy priesthood, to offer spiritual
sacrifices to God through Jesus Christ.
I PETER 2:5 ESV

If you've ever heard the expression "A rolling stone gathers no moss," then you will probably understand the concept of "sailing stones" found in a remote area of Death Valley, California. These heavy stones etch long tracks behind them across a dried lake bed known as Racetrack Playa. The stones, which range in size from several ounces to hundreds of pounds, seem to travel along the desert ground without human or animal intervention. No one has ever claimed to have actually seen them move, but the trails behind the stones seem to suggest that they do indeed move. In 2014 scientists were able to capture the stones' movements using time-lapse photography. What the camera revealed was a propelling force of ice, water, and wind. Rains would collect, freezing overnight to create a slick surface that would thaw the next day. Winds would then break down the ice sheet, melting, with the effect of propelling the stones forward across the lake bed.

FAITH CHECK

"A rolling stone gathers no moss" is a proverb with a bit of advice for people who cannot seem to settle in one place for long. Lichens and mosses grow slowly in stable environments, never on rolling stones. Some people sail through life because they fear settling in one place for too long, or staying with a job or in a relationship, often avoiding responsibilities and the cares of everyday life. But fear and faith are as incompatible as rolling stones and moss. Trusting in God, the Rock of your salvation, is the right move.

If you want to go fast,
go alone. If you want
to go far, go together.

–AFRICAN PROVERB

WRESTLING WITH GRACE

So Jacob named the place Peniel (the face of God),
saying, "For I have seen God face to face,
yet my life has not been snatched away."
GENESIS 32:30 AMP

We've seen it all in the world of wrestling, from Hulk Hogan to guys wearing masks and lucha libre stretchy pants. But the strangest match in the history of the world occurred outside of Canaan in the middle of the night. After a twenty-year absence, Jacob was on his way home with his wives and children. He was sweating bullets that Esau, the brother he had wronged, would seek revenge. With that worry on his mind, Jacob couldn't sleep and suddenly found himself wrestling a stranger under the starry sky. At some point before dawn, maybe when the stranger had him in a headlock, he realized that he was wrestling with God Himself. "When He saw that he did not prevail against him, He touched the socket of his hip; and the socket of Jacob's hip was out of joint..." (Genesis 32:25 NKJV). Now to be clear, Jesus could have totally whooped Jacob fair and square. If all He ever had to do to win was touch Jacob's hip, you know He could have yawned and knocked Jacob over with His pinkie finger any time He wanted. But the timing was right. God's timing.

FAITH CHECK

Before that match, Jacob did what he always did, connived his way out of sticky situations. But Jesus rassled the supplanter out of Jacob that night and Jacob walked away with a new name, "Israel," and God's blessing and a renewed faith.

Sometimes you win,
sometimes you learn.

★

SHEKINAH

I am the light of the world.
Whoever follows Me will never walk in darkness,
but will have the light of life.
JOHN 8:12 NIV

The time we seem to appreciate light the most is when the power suddenly cuts off. The darkness is truly overwhelming when you are fumbling around for a flashlight or a candle. These are the moments you are most likely to stub your toe on a baseboard or trip over a child's toy. Without light, we would all be stumbling about with no idea which direction we're headed and we'd have no idea of the dangers ahead of or around us. Jesus said that whoever walks in the darkness doesn't know where they are going. However, He promises that those who follow the "Light of the World" will not walk in darkness but have the light of life (John 8:12 ESV). God covers Himself in light as if it were a garment (Psalm 104:2). God's children are children of the light (John 12:36). And did you know that there is not a speck of darkness in God? In fact, darkness cannot exist in His presence. "Even the darkness is not dark to you; the night is bright as the day, for darkness is as light with you" (Psalm 139:12 ESV). Those who follow God walk in the light as He is in the light (I John 1:7).

FAITH CHECK

Each day, from the first blush of dawn, the sun climbs higher and higher until it is at its brightest at solar noon. At that point, a vertical stick in the ground will cast no shadow. If you're tired of fumbling around in the darkness, follow the light and stick with it.

The sun won't shine until
you put the umbrella away.

SWEET EVERYTHINGS

*Your hair is like a flock of goats leaping down
the slopes of Gilead. Your teeth are like a flock of
shorn ewes that have come up from the washing.*
SONG OF SOLOMON 4:1–2 ESV

Nothing can bring up your lunch like having to listen to an overly lovey-dovey couple repeat their romantic pet names for one another in public. Some couples are fond of calling one another affectionate names like Pookie, Sweet Pea, Pumpkin, Cowboy, Snuggle-kins, Numero Uno, Teddy Bear, and Tater Tot. Back in the sixties Sonny and Cher called one another Babe, but today young couples call each other Bae, a shortened form of Babe. In the South, however, folks are particular and maybe a little peculiar about what they call one another. Most of our pet names and nicknames begin life in a big bowl of sugar. We call one another Honey, Sugar, Sweetie, Buttercup, Cupcake, Peach, and Muffin. And if we get tired of those pet names we tack another word or two onto them. Sweetie becomes Sweetie-pie, Sugar-pie, Honey-pie, Honey-bunch, Honey-bun, or Honeybee. But there are other names like Tootsie and Bubba and Shug, and Sissy, Missy, and Beau. If you live in the South, chances are good you know someone by one of those names.

FAITH CHECK

In a world where people use cuss words like commas, isn't it nice to hear kind and affirming words instead? Words that make you feel warm and gooey inside? And maybe a little sugary. "Kind words can be short and easy to speak but their echoes are truly endless" (Mother Teresa).

Sure as the vine twines
'round the stump, you are
my darlin' sugar lump.

PARTNERS IN TIME

Therefore what God has joined together,
let no one separate.
MATTHEW 19:6 NIV

wise man once said that there are three kinds of men who don't understand women: young, old, and middle-aged. Many women would agree with that assessment, but many men would say that women don't understand them any better. Men and women seem to be wired differently, but is that a bad thing? And what's the alternative? If couples were alike in every way, there would either be too much conversation or not enough, too much emotion or too little. The truth is, men and women are most attracted to partners who differ from them. A quiet individual might appreciate the excitement of being around an energetic, vivacious person. A good conversationalist might enjoy being around a good listener. Our differences can aggravate us at times, but they do challenge and stimulate us to learn and to grow in our relationships as well.

FAITH CHECK

In marriage two individual people can become one terrible couple or one terrific couple. We can waste a lot of time and effort drawing lines in the sand or we can instead draw closer to God and one other and cross life's finish line together. Maybe the goal isn't to try and understand one another, or to moan about how different we are, but to embrace and blend our differences into a harmonious and beautiful union. A marriage with Christ at the center is a faithful force to be reckoned with.

Some people ask the secret of our long marriage. We take time to go to a restaurant two times a week. A little candlelight dinner, soft music, and dancing. She goes Tuesdays, I go Fridays.

—HENNY YOUNGMAN

GATES OF PEARL

Nothing unclean will ever enter it,
nor anyone who does what is detestable or false,
but only those who are written in the Lamb's book of life.
REVELATION 21:27 ESV

In the Old Testament, walls were built for protection from wild animals and to protect the inhabitants of the city from outside attack from other tribes or nations. Every city of substance had a wall or natural protective barrier surrounding it. The walls of Jericho fell when Joshua followed God's specific instructions to have the people march around the wall of the city, blow trumpets, and shout (Joshua 6:1–27). God called upon Nehemiah to rebuild the walls of Jerusalem. He obeyed and the people were blessed (Nehemiah 2:20). Prisons have walls to keep people from getting out. We live in homes surrounded by walls and ceilings to protect us from the weather, to give us privacy, and to make us feel secure from intruders. There is a high wall with gates around heaven as well with angels guarding each gate. "The twelve gates were twelve pearls; each individual gate was of one pearl" (Revelation 21:21 NKJV). Makes you wonder what kind of ginormous oysters could make pearls big enough for those gates.

FAITH CHECK

In the end, after death and Hades are cast into the lake of fire (Revelation 20:14-15), the pearly gates in the new heaven on the new earth will remain open forever in perpetual light. And the redeemed of the Lord will go in and out, bringing the glory and honor of the nations to the Lord.

May you always have walls
for the winds, a roof for
the rain, tea beside the fire,
laughter to cheer you, those
you love near you, and all
your heart might desire.

–IRISH BLESSING

THE GIFT OF WATER

Therefore with joy you will draw water
from the wells of salvation.
ISAIAH 12:3 NKJV

Over 70 percent of the earth's surface is covered with water. And up to 60 percent of the human adult body is composed of it. It is essential to our survival. A human being can live for about three weeks without food but perish in less than a week without water.

God uses water to protect. It flows throughout Scripture. God parted the Red Sea for the Israelites so they could escape Pharaoh's army (Exodus 14:1–21). He used water to purify, deliver, and destroy in the Great Flood of Noah (Genesis 6:17). He also uses water to heal, as in the story of Naaman the Syrian, who was healed from leprosy in the waters of the Jordan (II Kings 5:1–14). The Pool of Bethesda was known for annual miracles (John 5:1–9). The prophet Elisha healed a town's toxic water supply, with the effect of preventing death and healing miscarriages and barrenness (II Kings 2:19–22). But best of all, Jesus makes it clear to us that He is the Living Water. He told the woman at the well, "Everyone who drinks this water will be thirsty again, but whoever drinks the water I give them will never thirst" (John 4:13–14 NIV).

FAITH CHECK

Jesus tells us that the righteous are to give drink to those who are thirsty. "I was thirsty and you gave me drink" (Matthew 25:35–40 ESV). When we offer others the gift of living water, we are giving them the gift of eternal life. "Except a man be born of water and of the Spirit, he cannot enter into the kingdom of God" (John 3:5 KJV).

Come to the living waters!
Why will ye thirsty be? The
fountain of life is flowing,
is flowing now for thee.

–J. H. ALLEMAN

19
THE LORD OF HOSTS

Now King David was told,
"The LORD has blessed the household of Obed-Edom
and everything he has, because of the ark of God.
II SAMUEL 6:12 NIV

When family members or friends are staying with you for a spell, hosting involves a lot of prep work before they arrive. You put fresh sheets on the guest beds. Bathrooms must be spick-and-span unless you want your guests to wear flip-flops in the shower. Guest towels appear from the linen closet along with those teeny tiny fragrant bath soaps. And if your house isn't in tip-top shape, that means a floor-to-ceiling cleanup effort. But cleanup is only part of the prep. Meal planning is important. Breakfast, lunch, dinner, desserts, and snacks. Beverages too. And grocery shopping. But just imagine if you were suddenly called upon to host the Ark of the Covenant in your home. How would you prepare for that kind of visit?

FAITH CHECK

When King David was transporting the Ark on an ox cart to Jerusalem, the oxen stumbled and, in spite of God's warnings, a man named Uzzah reached out to steady it and died instantly. David was fearful of bringing the Ark into the city so he chose the nearby home of Obed-Edom to host it. For three months, everything and everybody in the house of Obed-Edom was greatly blessed. Hosting the Ark changed the family in every possible way. Afterwards, Obed-Edom and his family decided to become a blessing to God. They moved to Jerusalem and he and his many descendants continued serving as doorkeepers to the Ark, as well as gatekeepers, musicians, keepers of the storehouse, and more.

A guest is a jewel on the cushion of hospitality.

–REX STOUT

★

TOP TEN
"MUSTS"
FOR EVERY
CHURCH
HOSTESS

1. Know how to throw together a casserole on a moment's notice (Matthew 9:23 THE MESSAGE).

2. People can't get enough of congealed salads. Make sure you have a license to carry a congealed salad...to church.

3. Own lots of Tupperware. You can't have enough plasticware.

4. Deviled eggs belong on the Lord's banqueting table.

5. Print your name on your Pyrex or it belongs to the church.

6. Keep a trinity of these beverages in abundance: sweet tea, lemonade, and coffee. The church is always thirsty.

7. Remember, microwaving is not a sin.

8. Velveeta is a miracle of chemistry that belongs on the table at every church supper.

9. Two words. Dump Cake.

10. Own the cutest casserole cozies in the whole church. Or world.

RECIPE: STRAWBERRY JELLO SALAD

The appeal of congealed strawberry salad is that you can keep all the ingredients in your fridge and pantry for use at a moment's notice.

INGREDIENTS:

- 6 oz package of strawberry JELLO
- 1 cup boiling water
- 20 oz. frozen strawberries
- 20 oz can crushed-pineapple, drained well
- 3 medium bananas sliced
- ½ cup chopped pecans
- 16 oz sour cream

DIRECTIONS:

Whisk together gelatin and boiling water in a large non-metallic mixing bowl until the gelatin is dissolved. Add 20 oz can crushed pineapple, drained (do not use fresh), sliced bananas, frozen strawberries, and pecans. Mix well. Pour 1/2 of mixture into a 9x13 baking dish. Place in fridge to set for 20 minutes to half an hour. Set aside rest of gelatin but do not chill. When first layer is set, top with sour cream. Add rest of gelatin, smooth to the edges of the pan. Chill in fridge for two hours or overnight before slicing and serving.

SOURCE: ADAPTED FROM

https://southerndiscourse.com/strawberry-jello-salad/

20

THE LATTER AND
THE FORMER RAIN

Fear the LORD our God, that giveth rain,
both the former and the latter, in His season.
JEREMIAH 5:24 KJV

Farmers know when a bad cloud comes up, they're fixing to have a gully washer. But the rains in Israel only came twice a year for farmers. Israel was not located near abundant sources of water like the Nile or the Euphrates, probably because God wanted them to depend solely on Him to provide all the water they needed. The former rains, or autumn rains, which fall October through November, are gentle showers that soften the ground for planting. But the latter are spring rains, March through April, and these rains come down harder and can cause flooding and destruction. But in James 5:7 we see the comparison of the former and latter rains to the Spirit of God. "Be patient, then, brothers and sisters, until the Lord's coming. See how the farmer waits for the land to yield its valuable crop, patiently waiting for the autumn and spring rains" (NIV). These rains represent God's provision and grace to us, just as the rains provided water for people, crops, and animals to survive throughout the year.

FAITH CHECK

God has an abundance of blessings in store for us. He promises that He will pour out His Spirit on all flesh in the last days (Acts 2:17–21), an outpouring on all God's people from every nation and tongue. Just as the former rains prepared the land for seed and the latter rains for harvest, God will rain down His Spirit on us in the last days and bring in an abundance of souls to His glory.

If you have had grace once, the Lord has more for you. Do you suppose that because He gave you the former rain He has emptied the bottles of heaven?

–CHARLES SPURGEON

★

21

THE BLOOD COVENANT

It is the blood that makes atonement by the life.
LEVITICUS 17:11 ESV

Deals between people who trust each other can be sealed with spit on the palm and a slap on the hand. In the business world, people sign contracts that are enforced by the court system. In the Old Testament two parties would "cut a covenant" with one another. Literally. They would sacrifice animals and cut them up and mirror the parts on the ground. They would then walk the path between the blood sacrifice and say, "May this be done to me if I do not keep this oath." Abraham was old and had no heir so he went before the Lord and told him that he planned to leave his estate to his servant (Genesis 15). But God reminded him of an earlier promise that he would have a son of his own flesh for an heir, and further, that his descendants would be as numerous as the stars and have a land of promise to live in. To seal this oath, God instructed Abraham to arrange a covenant sacrifice. But instead of having them swear the covenant together, God walked the path *alone*, appearing as a "smoking oven," which is symbolic of a pillar of cloud by day and a pillar of fire by night. God offered Abraham a glimpse of how He would help, protect, and comfort all of Abraham's promised descendants in the time of the Exodus.

FAITH CHECK

God alone, not Abraham, promised to give His life in the event the contract was breached, for there was and is no one greater for God to swear by than Himself (Hebrews 6:13–18). But the ultimate blood covenant was offered by the Son of God, Jesus Christ (Luke 22:20).

God doesn't want us to
have rigid rituals with Him.
In the new covenant, He is
more interested in having
a relationship with us.

—JOSEPH PRINCE

YOU CAN RUN BUT...

Where can I go from Your Spirit?
Or where can I flee from Your presence?
PSALM 139:7 NKJV

Toddlers love to play hide-and-seek, but it's super adorable when they cover their eyes with their sweet little hands and believe they are invisible to those seeking them. Adam and Eve hid from God after they sinned and suddenly discovered they were naked, but Scripture says, "No creature is hidden from his sight, but all are naked and exposed to the eyes of him to whom we must give account" (Hebrews 4:13 ESV). Some people think that God can't hear them. But God heard His disciple Thomas say, "Unless I see in His hands the marks of the nails, and put my finger into the mark of the nail prints, and put my hand into His side, I will not believe" (John 20:25 AMP). Others believe that God doesn't know what they're thinking. But Psalms 139:4 confirms that "even before a word is on my tongue, behold, O LORD, you know it altogether" (ESV). Acting like you're perfect before God is like dressing up for an x-ray.

FAITH CHECK

Besides making us vulnerable, sin is like a filthy smudge that makes us feel too dirty to approach God, even to repent. But God knows everything, the temptations that led you to sin, the sins you committed, and the consequences you endured. Get right with God and He will take care of what's left.

God has a mind like a steel trap. My mind is more like a steel sieve.

—ROBIN TOMPKINS

★

❰ 23 ❱
WHAT THEY THINK

If the world hates you,
keep in mind that it hated Me first.
JOHN 15:18 NIV

People can get tired from jumping to so many conclusions. Yet that's all some folks do. We see people jumping to conclusions every day on television. We read it. We hear it on the radio. We see it on the Internet. And sometimes conclusions jump out of our own mouths. The Bible categorizes this behavior as a path to folly. "He that answereth a matter before he heareth it, it is folly and shame unto him" (Proverbs 18:13 KJV). In the real world, the obvious thing to do is to go straight to the person and ask them to tell their side of the story. A dedicated news reporter would go even further, interviewing other witnesses and gathering facts through research. In this crazy convoluted world we have to decide whether we want to be independent thinkers or go with the herd. The mob rules when people tickle our ears and tell us what they want us to know, and when we allow our emotions to tell us what to think. And the mob wins when we value someone else's word more than we value the truth. The real truth is in God's Word (John 17:17).

FAITH CHECK

The only exercise some people get is running their mouth, jumping to conclusions, and pushing their luck. Things are often not what they appear to be. Take the time and effort you would want others to put into searching for the truth about you, and do what is right even when no one else does.

If you follow the crowd
you might get lost in it.

★

24
OIL OF GLADNESS

Then Mary took a pound of very costly oil of spikenard,
anointed the feet of Jesus, and wiped His feet with her hair.
JOHN 12:3 NKJV

In ancient times oil of spikenard was greatly valued as perfume, incense, and medicine. Grown in the Himalayan mountains of India and Nepal, spikenard oil was a rare, imported product. This incense oil was offered at the "Altar of Incense" in the time of the tabernacle and the first and second Jewish temples. And it was at the altar of incense that an angel appeared to Zacharias and told him that he and his wife, Elisabeth, would have a son and his name would be John (Luke 1:11), better known as John the Baptist. When Mary of Bethany, Lazarus's sister, broke open an expensive alabaster vial of nard and anointed Jesus, Judas had a hissy fit followed by a self-righteous rant. He estimated that the extravagant gift poured over Jesus's feet could have fed the poor. Did Judas really care about the poor? Hardly. He had charge of the moneybag and Jesus knew that Judas regularly helped himself to it (John 12:6). Instead Jesus praised Mary, saying that she had put aside this perfume for the day of His burial and that wherever the gospel is preached throughout the world, what Mary did would also be told, in memory of her (Mark 14:9).

FAITH CHECK

Mary desired no other place in this world than to be at the feet of Jesus, and it was His feet that she anointed and wiped clean with her own hair. She offered incense over the Lamb of God who would soon take away the sins of the world.

Let your thoughts be psalms, your prayers incense, and your breath praise.

—CHARLES SPURGEON

25

THIS WAY OUT

Uzziah slept with his fathers, and they buried him
with his fathers in the burial field that belonged
to the kings, for they said, "He is a leper."
II CHRONICLES 26:23 ESV

Uzziah was a good king of the Old Testament who reigned for fifty-two years. He trusted God and was victorious over many tribes and nations. He constructed towers, dug wells, built up his army with weapons, and invented many devices of war to protect Jerusalem. It is thought that he and his men invented a type of catapult before the Greeks or Romans. But then one day Uzziah started to become a legend in his own mind. "He was marvelously helped, till he was strong" (II Chronicles 26:15 ESV). He got so puffed up with pride he decided to fulfill the office of priest and burn incense on the altar. But God did not allow men to combine the offices of king, priest, and prophet. When the priests confronted the king, he was furious instead of repentant, so God struck Uzziah with leprosy. Even in death his body was still considered unclean and was buried in the king's field nearby, not in the tombs of the kings. Thankfully, the blood of Christ saves, heals, protects, and delivers us eternally, cleansing us once and for all from sin.

FAITH CHECK

A prideful king went into the temple and a humble leper shamefully scurried out. Pride and an unrepentant heart have eternal consequences. The offices of priest, prophet, and king would one day be fulfilled, combined in One who was still to come, Jesus Christ, the Messiah. "My grace is sufficient for you, for my power is made perfect in weakness" (II Corinthians 12:9 ESV).

He ate and drank the
precious words,
His spirit grew robust;
He knew no more
that he was poor,
Nor that his frame
was dust.

–EMILY DICKINSON
★

26
LATE BLOOMERS

He has also planted eternity in the human heart.
ECCLESIASTES 3:11 AMP

Two of the most important days of our lives are the day we are born and the day we die. But many of us would include the day we find out why we exist. We seem to be hard-wired with such a longing, a sense of divine purpose. Some people are born knowing what they want to do in life. Others find out while they are still young and have long, successful careers. Still others don't discover their unique gifts and talents until they are long in the tooth, but they manage to succeed anyway. Grandma Moses didn't start painting until she was in her late seventies, and her American primitive paintings were shown in the Museum of Modern Arts in New York. Laura Ingalls Wilder was forty-three when she started writing her autobiography, which became her beloved Little House series. Ever referred to a thesaurus in school? Peter Mark Roget was a doctor, lecturer, and inventor who suffered from depression. At sixty-one he found a way to cope with it. He found that he enjoyed making lists, creating a catalog of words organized by their meanings.

FAITH CHECK

The most important reason we are all here on earth is to know God and to make Him known to others. And He uses our unique gifts, talents, and skills to share the truth and minister to people. Some of us bloom later in life. God prepares our hearts before anyone ever hears the gospel. "No one can say 'Jesus is Lord,' except by the Holy Spirit" (I Corinthians 12:3 NIV).

Ever since I made
tomorrow my favorite day
I've been uncomfortable
looking back.

—PAUL HARVEY

★

THE HOUSE OF THE SOUL

*For instance, we know that when these bodies of ours
are taken down like tents and folded away,
they will be replaced by resurrection bodies in heaven—
God-made, not handmade—and we'll never have
to relocate our "tents" again.*
II CORINTHIANS 5:1-2 THE MESSAGE

The very first thing most folks do when they go camping is pitch the tent. Sometimes you have your own small pup-style tent and other times there's a mega family-sized tent to wrestle with. Some folks prefer glamping in an RV to tent life. Whatever your tent looks like, it is no more than a temporary dwelling place, not your real home. Our bodies here on earth are temporary dwelling places as well. The tabernacle, or "Tent of the Congregation," was a tent that temporarily served as God's dwelling place here on earth but was a mere shadow of things to come because it was patterned after God's spiritual tabernacle in heaven. The apostle Paul was a tentmaker on the side and would have well understood the notion of our earthly tents being folded up and put aside. Our time here on this planet is timed and temporary. After we die we will go to a house not built by mortal hands, whose architect is God Himself. "Knowing that shortly I must put off this my tabernacle, even as our Lord Jesus Christ hath shewed me" (II Peter 1:14 KJV).

FAITH CHECK

When believers die, they leave their earthly tents behind and move into their permanent home, their eternal house with God forever. There will be no more temptations, violence, no sickness or disease, no decay or corruption, no exhaustion or loneliness, and no pain. No more death, and definitely no more tears.

That camping weekend
was *in tents*.

★

BENTO BOX FAITH

Their loyalty is divided between God and the world.
JAMES 1:8 NLT

If you've ever had lunch in a school cafeteria or eaten frozen dinner cuisine, camped, flown on an airline in the sixties, savored an MRE, consumed five-star hospital food, or dined at a Japanese restaurant, you might have had a meal in a Bento-type box. The nifty compartment trays contain everything you need for a healthy, well-balanced meal. Plus, there's something kind of fun about eating from compartments where the Salisbury steak gravy is contained in a detention pond and the gelatin can't creep its way into the soggy green beans.

We tend to compartmentalize our faith this way too. These are the things I'm believing God for. *These are the things I can do on my own. This section holds my answered prayers. This section holds my unanswered prayers. These are the Bible truths I'm expected to believe as a Christian. These are the other things I secretly believe that are contrary to my faith. These are my doubts. These are my fears. This compartment holds my unforgiveness. This one holds my secular life. This one holds my church life. This one holds my money and possessions. This one, my secret sins.*

FAITH CHECK

But God wants us to be whole and wholly His (I Thessalonians 5:23). We cannot separate our lives into comfortable little Bento Box compartments that enable us to live as we please. Our hearts pump blood to our entire body, bringing lifegiving oxygen and nutrients. When we ask Jesus into our heart, our heart conveys His blood to the whole of our being and brings forth life eternal.

God wants full custody,
not just weekend visits.

★

29

JUDGE NOT

Let justice roll down like waters,
and righteousness like an ever-flowing stream.
AMOS 5:24 ESV

nyone who has ever been accused of something they did not do is painfully aware of the hurt and helplessness of being forced into such an excruciating situation. Accusations tarnish an individual's good name and reputation. Unvalidated claims also wound and damage that person's family members, occupation, relationships, credibility, and status in the community they live in. People assume that if there is an accusation against someone there must be a ring of truth to it. However, believers should remember that the accuser of the brethren is Satan himself. We should not be a part of any such mob mentality when we hear of someone being accused. James 1:19–20 says, "Let every person be quick to hear, slow to speak, slow to anger; for the anger of man does not produce the righteousness of God" (ESV). Every person should be treated as you would also want to be treated. Innocent until proven guilty, not by hearsay or potentially false evidence. And certainly not by comments on social media or in the court of public opinion.

FAITH CHECK

God's truth will always triumph over Satan's lies. What else should we expect of the enemy? He is a liar and always will be. Yet fellow believers too often join him. Instead of truth telling, or discipling, or praying for, or forgiving, they attack God's elect with blind furor and enthusiasm. "Who shall bring any charge against God's elect? It is God who justifies" (Romans 8:33 ESV).

Never try to destroy someone's life with a lie when yours could be destroyed by the truth.

MEANING OF "NEWSPAPER"

"The word "newspaper" is derived not from the word "new," but from N-E-S-W (as in a compass) which it was usual in old times to put at the head of a periodical publication, indicating that the information was derived from the four corners of the globe."

SOURCE: ADAPTED FROM: 1847 Old Farmer's Almanac

https://www.almanac.com/fact/meaning-newspaper

30

CRAZY LIKE A FOX

*Those who look to Him for help will be radiant with joy;
no shadow of shame will darken their faces.*
PSALM 34:5 NLT

avid was on the run from Saul because Saul wanted David to examine the radishes. When you're running for your life, you don't always think things through. Which is the reason David sought refuge in Gath. If you remember, a certain giant named Goliath had come from that city, the giant David had killed. And it didn't help that David was carrying Goliath's sword either! The people of the city had heard the songs of praise about David, "Saul has slain his thousands, and David his tens of thousands" (I Samuel 21:10 NIV). So David pulled out the insanity card and pretended he was certifiably cuckoo, likely an award-worthy performance because the Philistines believed his madman act. David escaped to the cave of Adullam, where about four hundred men joined him. Did David sin by pretending to be a drooling lunatic, or was he all the while praying his socks off that God would deliver him? We might never know this side of heaven. In spite of his escape, David was still a hunted man and at a low point in life, yet he chose to pray and trust in the Lord.

FAITH CHECK

David looked to God in his fear and affliction, knowing that God would transform his present attitude and eventually his situation. When we look to God, His radiance stays with us. It is evident on our faces and in our lives. "But we all, with unveiled face, beholding as in a mirror the glory of the Lord, are being transformed into the same image from glory to glory, just as by the Spirit of the Lord" (II Corinthians 3:18 NKJV).

Though this be madness,
yet there is method in it.

—WILLIAM SHAKESPEARE,
HAMLET

★

◀ 31 ▶
BITTERSWEET

They tried to give Him wine mixed with myrrh;
but He did not take it.
MARK 15:23 NASB

Myrrh comes from small thorny trees in Africa and the Arabian Peninsula. A resin described as both bitter and fragrant is derived from the trees, which are bruised to cause them to bleed resin that then coagulates into a waxy gum. The gum was valued as perfume and incense as well as antiseptic and pain-relief medicine. The Ishmaelite traders who carried Joseph away as a slave had camels loaded with spices, balm, and myrrh (Genesis 37:25). Myrrh was an ingredient in the sacred incense used in the first and second temples in Jerusalem. The three kings brought three gifts to baby Jesus, one of which was myrrh, symbolic of His death and burial (John 19:39). Jesus was offered wine and myrrh before His crucifixion. The name of the city of Smyrna is derived from "myrrh," a chief export of the city of Ephesus in ancient times. And Mary, the name of the mother of Jesus, is also derived from the word myrrh. Though she was blessed and highly favored to give birth to the Messiah, her mother's heart was pierced with grief over her beloved son.

FAITH CHECK

Myrrh trees must be bruised to bring out the resin, the life blood of the tree that releases the fragrance. Jesus Christ hung on a tree for us. He was bruised for our iniquities (Isaiah 53:5). Messiah and Christian both mean "Anointed One." When you are crushed, do you turn to the Lord? Your trust and praise send a sweet fragrance to God, a sweet savor of sacred incense.

Prayer is a perfume to
our soul and a fragrance
that pleases God.

★

WHO RULES THE ROOST?

I will set no worthless thing before my eyes.
PSALM 101:3 NASB

Roosters are fierce barnyard protectors of their flocks, but some people manage to raise them as prized pets with catchy names like Gregory Peck or Rooster Cogburn. However, American statesman Dean Acheson expressed a more practical opinion of them when he said, "Roosters are not known for their charm." A rooster is all business. He lives to patrol the barnyard with an eye to protecting the flock and ensuring the survival of his offspring. Even as a rooster pecks at the dirt for food he is constantly scanning the sky or side-eyeing the perimeter for potential predators. Vigilant and suspicious, a rooster sounds a warning the moment he spots danger and will defend the flock to the death if need be.

FAITH CHECK

Are we as watchful when it comes to protecting our flock? A rooster quickly recognizes a threat or a predator approaching, but are we as diligent about threats to our family that come in ways we don't expect? Electronics can invite violence, impure sexual content, profanity, and more into our home roosts daily through television, radio, Internet, social media, and video games, yet sometimes we ignore the dangers or believe we are somehow immune to the effects on our spiritual life. Some content is good and necessary to our daily lives, but parents must be vigilant in protecting those who are precious to them from content that is threatening or harmful. The enemy cannot entertain us when we refuse to entertain him.

Trying to sneak a fastball
past Hank Aaron is
like trying to sneak the
sunrise past a rooster.

–JOE ADCOCK

★

❖ 33 ❖
THE FAITH BATTERY

Even if our gospel is veiled,
it is veiled to those who are perishing,
whose minds the god of this age has blinded,
who do not believe, lest the light of the gospel
of the glory of Christ, who is the image of God,
should shine on them.

II CORINTHIANS 4:3-4 NKJV

pastor of a small church called all the young children to the pulpit one Sunday. Then he brought out a lantern and asked which of them knew what it was. Though all guessed correctly, he shook his head and explained that it was a solar lantern. He pointed at the solar cells on top and told them that the lantern had a battery cell on the top portion, and during the day when the sun was shining, the battery stored up the sun's energy. Then at night the lantern would shine in the darkness because of the energy it saved up during the day. He explained that faith is a lot like a solar lantern. When our faith is strong and we pray and seek God, it's like we're storing up power in our faith battery. Then when we go through hard times, when things seem hopeless and dark, the light of our faith shines in the darkness around us and gives us comfort and hope.

FAITH CHECK

How many of us sit shivering in fear and despair without hope or light to guide us through dark times in our lives? The Bible contains all the light we need to find our way in this world. In it are God's words of hope and life, testimonies of faith, and God's promises to us. Many people who turn its pages have turned their hearts and lives to Him.

We are told to let our light shine, and if it does we won't have to tell anybody it does. Lighthouses don't have to fire cannons to call attention to their shining. They just shine.

—DWIGHT L. MOODY

34

THE FRIENDSHIP
OF THE LORD

The secret of the LORD is with those who fear Him,
and He will show them His covenant.
PSALM 25:14 NKJV

Who do you tell your secrets to? If you're smart, you will spill the tea of your life with good close friends, people with a proven track record of trustworthiness. If not, you'll be sorry. God is like that too. When you walk with Him, He walks right alongside you and communicates His feelings, teaches you, and even shares His secrets with you. Abram was an attentive host to three angels who visited him at his camp. As they were leaving, however, he noticed that they were headed toward Sodom, the city where his nephew Lot lived, and that worried him. So God spoke to Abram. "Shall I hide from Abram what I am about to do?" (Genesis 18:17 NIV). God had planned on telling Abram from the get-go that He was about to blot out Sodom and Gomorrah, otherwise He wouldn't have sent the three angels to Abram's tent. God wants to speak to us in confidential counsel and communion and does so mostly through His Word, the Bible, in order to share the gospel with others, to warn and prepare us for future events, and to bring us to repentance.

FAITH CHECK

The entire Book of Revelation is all about God sharing a big secret with us about what is about to happen in the end times. "Behold! I tell you a mystery. We shall not all sleep, but we shall all be changed" (I Corinthians 15:51 ESV). He tells us precisely what to look for as we approach the events that are to come, and He gives us signs to help us navigate. To understand. To prepare.

Heaven is not a figment of imagination. It is not a feeling or an emotion. It is not the "Beautiful Isle of Somewhere." It is a prepared place for a prepared people.

–DR. DAVID JEREMIAH

35

THE GREATEST STORY
NEVER TOLD

Sanctify the Lord God in your hearts: and be ready always
to give an answer to every man that asketh you a reason
of the hope that is in you with meekness and fear.
I PETER 3:15 KJV

There's an old Irish blessing that says, "Time is a great storyteller." Everyone has a life story. The old man in the hardware store, the young woman on a bicycle, the middle-aged mother whose story is etched across her forehead, the child sitting alone on the playground bench. If you are following the Lord, your story gets better and better with time because you hopefully remember all the answered prayers in your life. You remember all the times you cried out to God and He answered. If you don't remember, start writing everything down. Think back as far as you can and write down all those times God came to your rescue or answered your needs, or gave you the desire of your heart. God didn't do all that He has done in your life so you can keep it all to yourself and leave this earth without ever telling another soul. There are souls who need to hear your story.

FAITH CHECK

We all have a story worth telling to others. God says that our testimonies are powerful and life-changing. Sharing your testimony is showing others how the gospel of Jesus Christ has changed your life. The Word of God and your testimony are the strongest weapons against all the plans and evil purposes of the enemy. "They overcame him because of the blood of the Lamb and because of the word of their testimony, and they did not love their life even when faced with death" (Revelation 12:11 NASB).

But there is one thing
better than going to
heaven, and that is to
encourage at least one
other person to go with me.

—NICK VUJICIC

36

THE RESURRECTION PLANT

*All flesh is grass, and all its beauty is like the flower
of the field. The grass withers, the flower fades when the
breath of the LORD blows on it; surely the people are grass.*
ISAIAH 40:6-7 ESV

Ever go out of town for an extended vacay and forget to arrange for someone to water your houseplants? You come home to sorrowful sticks in the dirt and a slightly guilty feeling itching at you. Plants, like humans and animals and, let's be honest, every living thing on this planet, need water to survive. There's an odd plant called the Rose of Jericho, however, that redefines what's normal for survival. How many plants do you know of that can dry up to a mummified state and then come back like nothing happened? Yes, the Rose of Jericho can go from gorgeous green to tumbleweed and back again depending on the weather. A desert plant, the Rose of Jericho adapted itself to its climate over the years. In dry seasons its stems and seedpods curl into tight balls, which will only uncurl when exposed to moisture. In wet seasons, the plants put off little white flowers and seeds that germinate into new plants. If the seeds fall on poor soil, they wither and die. If the seeds fall on good soil, they grow and flourish. And the cycle begins again.

FAITH CHECK

The Rose of Jericho is also called the "resurrection plant" because of its unique ability to "come back from the dead." Christians for centuries have related this plant to the resurrection of Jesus Christ. We live. We have children. We grow old. We die. But earthly death has no hold over believers, for in Christ Jesus they will live again as new creations in glorified bodies.

Our Lord has written the promise of resurrection, not in books alone, but in every leaf in springtime.

–MARTIN LUTHER

37

NO SITTING DOWN
ON THE JOB

He said to them, "Why did you seek Me? Did you not know
that I must be about My Father's business?"
LUKE 2:49 NKJV

aiters and waitresses work hard for their money in both greasy diners and fancy restaurants. They are forever on their rubber-soled feet, nibbling a cracker packet lunch on the go or a "kitchen mistake" in between orders. Anyone who works on their feet all day looks forward to time in the break room so they can put their tootsies up and rest. Not so for the priests in the tabernacle, known also as the Tent of the Congregation by the children of Israel. The tabernacle was the portable earthly dwelling place of God on earth. Tabernacle priests could not sit when they wanted to because there were no chairs inside. Furniture was sparse to begin with: an altar, a large basin for washing, curtains, a table, the ark, and a lampstand. Why? The ministry of the Levitical priesthood was a continual work. "Every priest stands daily at his service, offering repeatedly the same sacrifices, which can never take away sins" (Hebrews 10:11 ESV).

FAITH CHECK

The priests in the tabernacle never sat. But Jesus, our High
Priest (Hebrews 7:13–17), finished the work when He gave His
life on the cross for us. The moment He said, "It is finished,"
there was nothing more to be done, no lights to tend, no more
sins to atone for. His blood on the altar paid for our sins once
and for all. And when Jesus ascended into heaven, He sat on
the right hand of the Father (Hebrews 10:12).

Work as if everything
depended upon your work,
and pray as if everything
depended upon your prayer.

—WILLIAM BOOTH

★

THE GLOOM IN THE ROOM

May the God of hope fill you with all joy and peace
as you trust in Him, so that you may overflow with hope
by the power of the Holy Spirit.
ROMANS 15:13 NIV

ave you ever met someone who's known as the gloom in the room? The "Eeyore" at the Super Bowl party? The one person who cannot look on the bright side to save their life? For someone like that, the glass is always half empty. The sun cannot shine brightly enough. "I'll probably fail my final exam. I entered the contest but there's no chance I'll win. No one wants to date me. I'm not smart enough. I'm ordinary. I'll never be able to save enough money to buy a house." Is failure the root of such a gloomy outlook on life? Negativity is like a shield, protecting the feelings and emotions of the person underneath it. Someone who has been hurt in the past. Maybe the person experienced devastating failures, or has bad childhood memories. Lack of hope cancels out motivation. The past, for whatever reason, was a disappointment. The now is unsatisfactory. So, for the pessimist, the future holds no promise. But God offers us a very different expectation through His Word, the Bible. "'For I know the plans I have for you,' declares the LORD, 'plans to prosper you and not harm you, plans to give you hope and a future.'" (Jeremiah 29:11 NIV).

FAITH CHECK

In his The Rest of the Story *radio show, American journalist Paul Harvey once said, "I've never seen a statue erected to a pessimist." The Debbie Downers and the Negative Neds of the world need to hear the good news from those who hope in the Lord and trust Him. That kind of enthusiasm is cheerfully contagious!*

It's not much of a tail,
but I'm sort of
attached to it.

—A. A. MILNE, *EEYORE*

39

UNDER THE BROOM TREE

Not by might, not by power, but by My Spirit,
says the LORD of Hosts.
ZECHARIAH 4:6 ESV

Elijah had experienced a great victory for God over Baal and his prophets, but he was now on the run from a very ticked-off Queen Jezebel. He was so depressed, despondent, and exhausted that he prayed to God that he might die. "It is enough," he said (I Kings 19:4). Maybe he thought that the victorious miracle of God the people had just witnessed would have sparked a revival or repentance. But it didn't and Elijah was down in the dumps. So God told him to go out and stand on the mountain and the Lord would pass by him. The wind howled around him and broke the rocks in pieces. The earth quaked, and a fire raged after that. But God did not choose to speak through these manifestations. He chose to speak to Elijah in a still small voice, the same voice that believers hear in their hearts today. God sometimes speaks in dramatic ways, but He mostly speaks to us in a gentle whisper that leads us to repentance, comforts us, guides us, and directs us on the path of righteousness. Later God showed Elijah that his faithful walk and daily ministry had borne much fruit. He'd succeeded for God in a great many ways but hadn't even noticed.

FAITH CHECK

Thankfully, we don't always get what we want. At a low point in his life, Elijah suffered a spiritual breakdown and wanted to die. But not long afterwards, God sent a chariot of fire in a whirlwind to take Elijah to heaven and Elijah didn't die at all (II Kings 2:11). Sometimes a no from God is a much better blessing.

It is the still, small voice
that the soul heeds, not the
deafening blasts of doom.

—WILLIAM DEAN HOWELLS

★

40

THE SKY IS FALLING!

About that day or hour no one knows, not even the angels in heaven, nor the Son, but only the Father.

MARK 13:32 NIV

Henny Penny is a European folk tale known in the United States as "Chicken Little" or "Chicken Licken." The story is about a panicky little chicken who believes the world is coming to an end because an acorn fell on his head, and he proclaims, "The sky is falling." Over the years, many people have announced the end of the world will happen on this day or that. Most of them use their "superior" knowledge to try and predict the day of Christ's return and, curiously enough, blame their math skills when things don't work out. But the most interesting end-of-the-world prediction happened in 1806 in England. "The Prophet Hen of Leeds" appeared to lay eggs with the message "Christ is Coming" on the eggshell. Somehow, many people were convinced that God would announce the Second Coming from a hen's bottom. However, it was soon discovered that the hen's owner was behind the cruel "yolk."

FAITH CHECK

In Jewish tradition, a couple enters a betrothal ceremony in which they are considered to be married but do not consummate the marriage or live together for one year. The groom prepares a place for the bride, but it is the father who tells the groom when it is time to return for his bride (John 14:3). One day when you least expect Him, Jesus will return for His bride, the church. Be ready.

94

Stop worrying about
the world ending today.
It's already tomorrow
in Australia.

–CHARLES M. SCHULTZ

THE WALKING DEATH

That if you confess with your mouth Jesus as Lord,
and believe in your heart that God raised Him
from the dead, you will be saved.
ROMANS 10:9 NASB

Zombie shows and movies can really make your liver quiver and the chill bumps rise. It's scary to imagine a world overrun with haints instead of saints. But here's something to think about: Before we are born again we are all dead spiritually. We look fine on the outside, but inside we are definitely not okay. We are born into a world of sin and are sinners who cannot remedy the situation we are in except by way of a Savior. Jesus Christ paid for our sins with His life and offers us the free gift of eternal life. When we ask Him into our heart, He rescues and redeems us from sin and gives us a new heart and a new life. The blood of Christ transforms us. Though we might look the same on the outside, we won't live our lives the same way afterwards. We won't think the way we did before, and we won't shamble around, wandering aimlessly through life. Instead, our lives will have meaning and purpose and we will hold onto the blessed hope of greater things to come.

FAITH CHECK

When Moses realized who he truly was, he refused to be called the son of Pharaoh's daughter anymore. His identity was with his God and with his people. When we realize who we are, that we are no longer bound by sin but are God's own children, we discover that God has also made us His heirs (Galatians 4:7 NIV).

When God saves a man, He is regenerating his heart, turns him into a new creature, and the evidence is this...he will live like a new creature and he will confess Christ.

–PAUL WASHER

THE HEAVENLY COUNTRY

As it is, they desire a better country, that is, a heavenly one.
Therefore God is not ashamed to be called their God,
for He has prepared for them a city.
HEBREWS 11:16 ESV

ots of young people are opting for tiny homes instead of the big ones the rest of us desire. They don't seem to mind being cramped into teensy-weensy spaces and enjoying all that tiny home togetherness that comes with the lifestyle. Give them a few years and a few kids, though, and they'll be hollering for more space, more privacy and "me" time. If you think about it, though, we all have our spaces. While our homes or apartments or condos come in all different sizes, they all have one thing in common: The place we live is the spot we call home sweet home. As the years pass and the kids grow and go, and we lag and sag, the time comes around for each of us to relocate to heavenly real estate. Did you know that the only land that Abraham and Sarah owned in the Promised Land was the Cave of Machpelah, the tomb their bodies were laid to rest in? (Genesis 23:9). Abram purchased the land for a burial place when his beloved wife Sarah died. He had chosen to uproot his family and servants and follow God, but only his descendants inherited the land.

FAITH CHECK

Believers greatly desire and long for a heavenly country.
Though this world is not our own, Jesus promises us that we
will each have a place of our own in heaven. And at some
point in life, when we are called to our heavenly home from
the little plot of land we live in or the resting spot we are
buried in, we will hear the sound of a trumpet and the words
"Come up here!" And we will truly be home sweet home.

Home is
where our story begins.

★

43

COME AGAIN ANOTHER DAY

The Lord God had not caused it to rain.
GENESIS 2:5 KJV

Can you imagine living in a world without rain? Yet there were no weather forecasters or rained-out picnics in Noah's day. The Bible says that Noah had never seen rain, much less torrential rain or destructive floods of water. Before the Great Flood, streams and rivers watered the plants as well as springs of water that flowed upward from under the earth to mist and hydrate the plants. So, Noah had to take God's Word in faith for this thing called "rain" and follow God's instructions to prepare for a dystopian event he could never even imagine (Genesis 6:5). "By faith Noah, being warned by God concerning events as yet unseen, in reverent fear constructed an ark for the saving of his household" (Hebrews 11:7 ESV). And God saved Noah and his family along with a menagerie of animals inside that huge ark constructed of wood.

FAITH CHECK

God made a covenant promise to us that He would never again destroy the earth with a flood. He sealed this promise with a bow of colors in the sky that could only appear with the presence of instability in the atmosphere known as rain—a rainbow. "I do set My bow in the cloud, and it shall be for a token of a covenant between Me and the earth (Genesis 9:13 KJV). When there is instability in the atmosphere of your life, remember that we are living arks for God to dwell in, holding the promise of eternal life with Him that those who believe will not perish.

There is but one Church in which men find salvation, just as outside the ark of Noah it was not possible for anyone to be saved.

–THOMAS AQUINAS

44
FORBID THEM NOT

From the lips of children and infants You, Lord,
have called forth Your praise.
MATTHEW 21:16 NIV

A new baby is a precious sight at family gatherings. Everyone vies to hold and coddle the little one and listen to its sweet coos. They all compete with one another as to who the baby most resembles. Then there are "knee babies," toddlers who are barely able to walk and are cute as all get-out. Toddlers and young children are called "crumb snatchers" because their tiny hands will come out of nowhere to snatch a cookie or cracker off your plate when you're not paying attention. But when children are a bit older, they're expected to mind their manners. If a son is getting a bit too fidgety or cutting up during a church service, his father will frown at him and say, "Boy, I'm about to cloud up and rain all over you!" Some people stick with the adage that children should be seen but not heard, but too much discipline can steal the sparkle from a child's eyes, and not enough can steal yours.

FAITH CHECK

The disciples got a bit annoyed when a crowd of people kept bringing their little ones to Jesus so He could lay hands on them. They wanted to lay hands on the kids and shoo them away! But Jesus did not like that attitude at all and quickly rebuked them. "Let the little children come to Me, and do not hinder them, for the kingdom of God belongs to such as these" (Mark 10:14 NIV). Instead of shushing and shooing children so much, maybe we should sit down and listen more and love on them, and guard that sweet sparkle in their eyes. Children aren't children forever.

Any kid will run
any errand for you,
if you ask at bedtime.

-RED SKELTON

❖ 45 ❖
FEELING POORLY

A cheerful heart is good medicine.
PROVERBS 17:22 NIV

Southerners have a unique way of describing various maladies. If Uncle Bubba has a hitch in his get-along, he's got a sore back or sciatica. If your great auntie is indisposed, she's feeling poorly, but only slightly. She's not on her deathbed. If, however, your aunt Vermale is sick as a dog, she's probably driving the porcelain bus, and her forehead is hotter than a possum in a wool sock. If your mama's "afflicted," she's having the hot flashes. Now, if you are "eat up" with something, that's generally not so good. You could have either a raging case of poison ivy or some wasting away kind of disease. If someone's "got the shuga," you can best believe they've got diabetes. Your cousin who hit the jug all his life has got himself a pickled liver, but if he's "tough as a pine knot" he might pull through. Or you might have a second cousin who's a mite "tetched in the head" ever since that mule kicked him. And if your grampa ain't right neither, he's likely got the dementia. If you ask these folks how they're doing, you'll get a whole range of answers from "I'd have to feel better to die," to "I'm worn slap out," or "I'm too weak to whip a gnat."

FAITH CHECK

Prayer is our most effective prescription from God for healing. Corrie Ten Boom once said, "Is prayer your steering wheel or your spare tire?" Prayer should be the first thing we do when we're sick, not the last. So if you're feeling poorly and look like something the dog buried under the porch, pray in faith. Jesus said, "All things are possible to him who believes" (Mark 9:23 NKJV).

For every ailment under
the sun, there is a remedy,
or there is none. If there be
one, try to find it; if there
be none, never mind it.

—MOTHER GOOSE

46

BLESSED IS HE

Hosanna to the Son of David!
Blessed is He who comes in the name of the Lord!
Hosanna in the highest!
MATTHEW 21:9 ESV

Palm Sunday or Passion Sunday is best known as the week before Easter, so named because of the palm branches people waved in the air and laid across Jesus's path in His triumphal entry into Jerusalem. The prophet Zechariah foretold this event. "See, your King comes to you, righteous and victorious, lowly and riding on a donkey, on a colt, the foal of a donkey" (9:9 NIV). In ancient times, palm branches were considered symbols of victory and triumph. However, the tradition of palm branches originates with the Jewish festival of Sukkoth, also known as Tabernacles or Booths, marking the end of the harvest time. Worshippers would wave willow, myrtle, and palm branches bundled together and recite Psalm 118, "O LORD, save now, we beseech You," followed by, "Blessed is the one who comes in the name of the LORD" (vv. 25–26 AMP).

FAITH CHECK

The people joyfully called out, "Hosanna!" on Palm Sunday, which means, "Save now!" They were hoping for a political leader, a worldly king who would overthrow the Romans, not the King of kings, the Messiah as foretold. The people didn't get what they thought they wanted. They got what they really needed. Jesus came first as the Lamb of God to take away the sins of the world, but He will return as the victorious Lion of Judah to execute judgment against evil (Revelation 19:14–16).

They would lay down their palms; He would lay down His life. A lot can change in a week.

–BOB GOFF

THE COOKIE LADY

Therefore go and make disciples of all nations,
baptizing them in the name of the Father
and of the Son and of the Holy Spirit.
MATTHEW 28:19 NIV

Born into a wealthy family in Virginia on December 12, 1840, Charlotte Digges Moon soon picked up the nickname Lottie. An educator, she joined her missionary sister in Tengchow, China, where she would live for the next thirty-nine years. In 1885 she decided to go inland to Pingtu where no missionary had been able to establish work. During the Boxer Rebellion, when Christians were suffering persecution, she dared not go into Pingtu by herself, so she acquired a covered chair on poles, the kind Chinese officials rode in, and dressed in a long robe, short coat, and large-rimmed glasses. She slicked back her hair and put on a hat similar to the type officials wore. Once there, she found thirteen Christians who had been brutally tortured and she was able to encourage and care for them. Lottie Moon was born with a silver spoon in her mouth, but she gave away all the silver and gold she had so that others might be born again. In the latter part of her life, she refused to eat while others around her were starving. When she finally passed away, Lottie was said to have weighed only fifty pounds.

FAITH CHECK

To reach the children of the villages, Lottie would bake little tea cakes for them. In time, the children began to call her "the cookie lady." Today, many families bake Lottie Moon cookies for Christmas in honor of her missionary work in China and to raise awareness and support of Christian missionary work all over the world.

Words fail to express my love for this holy book, my gratitude for its author, for His love and goodness. How shall I thank Him for it?

—LOTTIE MOON

RECIPE:
PLAIN TEA
CAKE

AS MADE BY LOTTIE MOON

INGREDIENTS:

- 3 teacups of sugar
- 1 teacup of butter
- 1 teacup of sour milk
- 4 pints of flour
- 3 eggs, well beaten
- 1/2 teaspoon of soda
- Flavor to taste. Roll thin.
- Bake in a quick oven.

ADAPTED RECIPE FOR TODAY'S COOKS

INGREDIENTS:

- 2 cups of flour
- 1/2 cup butter
- 1 heaping cup of sugar
- 1 well-beaten egg
- 1 tablespoon cream

DIRECTIONS:

Cream the butter and sugar. Add the egg and mix well. Add the flour and cream. Dust a board with flour. Roll the dough very thin. Cut cookies with a round cookie cutter. Place on a buttered or nonstick cookie sheet. Bake at 475 degrees for about 5 minutes.

SOURCE:

http://www.wmu.com/?q=article/national-wmu/lottie-moon-tea-cake-recipe

◀ 48 ▶
FAITHFUL THOMAS

Blessed are those who have not seen and yet have believed.
JOHN 20:29 NIV

Whenever anyone mentions Jesus's disciple Thomas, they always add the word "Doubting" before his name. Imagine how shameful it must have been for him to know that his greatest weakness was paraded before the world and added to his name on the front end! Now think about your greatest weakness being tacked on to your name. Hits home, doesn't it? When Jesus appeared to His disciples after He rose from the dead, Thomas wasn't there (John 20:25). So when they told him that Jesus had come for a visit, he probably scrunched his face to the side and said, "Right..." Fast forward eight days and Jesus appears again. This time, Thomas was there. The doors were locked and Jesus walked on in. After Jesus said, "Peace be with you," to the group, He turned to Thomas lickety-split and told him to place his fingers on the indentations in His hands and side. Thomas did and he exclaimed, "My Lord and my God!" Thomas believed when he saw the proof.

FAITH CHECK

Thomas asked honest questions. God appreciates our honesty because to be honest, He already knows what we're thinking. Jesus wasn't mad at Thomas. He was teaching him a valuable lesson about faith. Thomas was also called Didymus, which means twin, and at times we are all as double-minded as Thomas was. But the moment Thomas said those words, all doubts ceased in him about his Lord and Savior. The truth had truly set him free.

I believe though I do not comprehend, and I hold by faith what I cannot grasp with the mind.

—SAINT BERNARD

★

HIS SIGNET RING

"The glory of this present house will be greater than
the glory of the former house," says the LORD Almighty.
"And in this place I will grant peace."
HAGGAI 2:9 NIV

The prophet Haggai went to King Zerubbabel with a word from God that He would make Zerubbabel His "signet ring," a symbol of sovereign authority. Zerubbabel was to be the principal builder of the new temple. In the years since Nehemiah had rebuilt the walls, the people had become preoccupied with their own needs and comforts. And they weren't so thrilled with the replacement temple. Solomon had spared no expense in building the grand first temple. In contrast, the replacement temple was puny. But God promised them something better. "'In a little while I will once more shake the heavens and the earth, the sea and the dry land. I will shake all nations, and the desired of all nations will come, and I will fill this house with glory.... The silver is mine and the gold is mine,'" declares the LORD Almighty" (Haggai 2:6–8 NIV). The people were looking at the glory of the former temple, but God promised to fill the latter temple with a glory far greater than the cloud of God's Shekinah glory that had filled Solomon's temple.

FAITH CHECK

God has appointed us like Zerubbabel with all authority to go forth and make disciples of all nations (Matthew 28:18-19). This is our divine purpose, to share the good news of salvation with the whole world. God's people were told to rebuild the temple and He would send a greater glory. And 550 years later, Jesus Christ the Son of God walked through its doors.

You don't give God
authority over your life.
He has it, totally.

–JOHN PIPER

★

WIND AND WEATHERVANES

You know how to interpret the appearance of the sky,
but not the signs of the times!
MATTHEW 16:3 BEREAN

Do you know which way the wind is blowing? People in ancient times used to tie strings of cloth to the tops of structures for that very purpose. And then banners, which in Old English comes from the word *vane*, meaning "banner" or "flag." Weathervanes came next, complete with the four points of the compass and featuring a variety of decorative designs and curlicues. But the most prominent feature on weathervanes is often a rooster, known as a "weathercock," and goes all the way back to St. Peter. At the Last Supper Jesus told Peter, "Before the rooster crows today, you will deny me three times" (Luke 22:61 ESV), and Peter did just that, though he wept bitterly and mourned what he had done. Over the centuries, the rooster somehow became the symbol of the apostle Peter. In the ninth century, Pope Nicolas decreed that all churches had to display the rooster on their steeples or domes as a symbol of Peter's betrayal of Jesus. Like Doubting Thomas, Peter would suffer the association of his greatest failure with his name.

FAITH CHECK

Today, most weathervanes are purely decorative. We have access to accurate weather forecasts as close as our fingertips are to our electronic devices. As believers must heed what we read in our Bibles, be aware of the times we live in, and follow the lead of the Holy Spirit (I Corinthians 10:1–11 NIV).

When He returns is not
as important as the fact
that we are ready for Him
when He does return.

—A. W. TOZER

WEATHER
PROVERBS

- The higher the clouds, the finer the weather.

- If the goose honks high, fair weather. If the goose honks low, foul weather.

- When dew is on the grass, rain will never come to pass.

- Clear moon, frost soon.

- When clouds appear like rocks and towers, the earth is refreshed by frequent showers.

- Frogs croaking in the lagoon, means rain will come real soon.

- Doors and drawers stick before a rain.

- A year of snow, a year of plenty.

- Rainbow in the morning gives you fair warning.

- Ring around the moon? Rain real soon.

- Red sky at night, sailors delight. Red sky in morning, sailors take warning.

SOURCE:

Weather Folklore Weathervanes) https://www.almanac.com/content/weather-sayings-and-their-meanings

https://www.artofmanliness.com/articles/22-old-weather-proverbs-that-are-actually-true/

51

SPIRITUAL WARFARE

No weapon formed against you shall prosper,
and every tongue which rises against you
in judgment you shall condemn.
ISAIAH 54:17 NKJV

When you're hiking in the woods, have you ever tried to convince yourself that a bear won't bother you on the trail if you ignore it? Of course not. Bears will be bears. They are wild, unpredictable creatures and you are treading in their territory. Some people have the mistaken impression that believers live a life of ease and safety, without adversity or problems. But that is far from the truth. The enemy works double time and overtime to afflict and interfere with those who commit their lives to Christ. He prowls around looking for someone to destroy (I Peter 5:8). The good news, however, *is* the Good News. God has given us mighty and powerful weapons to defeat the enemy through the pulling down of strongholds (II Corinthians 10:4). We defeat the enemy through prayer, fasting, speaking God's Word over every situation, and trusting God, "Through You we push back our enemies; through Your name we trample our foes" (Psalm 44:5 NIV).

FAITH CHECK

Remember, there is no testimony without the test. When you get decked out in the full armor of God, the devil has to go through Jesus to get to you (Ephesians 6:10–18). The sword of the Spirit (Hebrews 4:12) is God's Word, which pierces and penetrates the plans and schemes of the enemy, yet heals and restores believers. The overcoming power God has given believers is not beyond our comprehension, it is beyond what most of us can imagine.

God never said
the weapons wouldn't form.
He said they
wouldn't prosper.

★

52

LOW COUNTRY LIVING

There is the sea, vast and spacious,
teeming with creatures beyond number—
living things both large and small.
PSALM 104:25 NIV

ow country living is a sunrise stroll on the beach to look for shells and sea glass. Saltwater and white sugar sand. Spanish moss hanging from live oaks, dripping dew on those who pass below. A place where weeping willow trees cascade, straddling both land and water. A captivating area along the South Carolina coast is known as the "Lowcountry," a charming coastal location with a unique culture, geography, cuisine, and more. On St. Helena island in South Carolina is a small white clapboard building known as the Coffin Point Praise House, built in antebellum days, a place for slaves to pray. Wealthy planters constructed fine churches for themselves in those days, but the slaves had only modest places to gather, small because the plantation owners feared large groups where rebellion might form. But little did the plantation owners know that a fearsome storm of war was brewing, one that would soon change everything.

FAITH CHECK

Singing was a big part of worship in the Coffin Point Praise House, and services most often ended with call-and-response rounds called "shouts." We have a call-and-response decision in our lives as well, the most important one we will ever make. The decision to ask Jesus in sets us all free from the law of sin and death. Whether you live on a majestic mountain or in a low country estuary, high on the hog or poor as a field mouse, the ground at the cross is level.

I was born and raised on a Carolina sea island and I carried the sunshine of the country, inked in dark gold, on my back and shoulders.

–PAT CONROY,
THE PRINCE OF TIDES

HIS LOVE

Greater love has no one than this:
to lay down one's life for one's friends.
JOHN 15:13 NIV

If you grew up in church, you definitely grew up singing "Jesus Loves Me." The popular song sweetly sung by little children is from a Christian hymn written by Anna Bartlett Warner (1927–1915), but the lyrics first appeared as a poem in her sister Susan's novel *Say and Seal*. In the novel, the "Jesus Loves Me" verses offer comfort to a dying child. In 1862, William Batchelder Bradbury added a tune and a chorus, "Yes, Jesus Loves Me," and the song became one of the most recognizable and popular Christian hymns worldwide. Though many believers know the song inside and out, how is it that we can so easily forget the song's simple message? A little girl or boy believes that Jesus loves them. Children will draw a heart shape and scribble an image of Jesus inside that precious heart. Children believe because the Bible tells them about the love of Christ. They know that they belong to God. They know that even though they are small, their God is big and strong and can do anything!

FAITH CHECK

Faith is being sure of what we hope for and certain of what we do not see. A humble and unpretentious faith is the childlike faith Jesus tells us about. "Truly I tell you, anyone who will not receive the kingdom of God like a little child will never enter it" (Luke 18:17 NIV). Without faith, it is impossible to please God, but most important of all, without faith we cannot have Jesus in our hearts, for by faith we believe (Hebrews 11:1-6).

Jesus loves me, this I know, for the Bible tells me so. Little ones to Him belong; they are weak, but He is strong. Yes, Jesus loves me! Yes, Jesus loves me!

—ANNA BARTLETT WARNER

AMONG THE MYRTLE TREES

They were stoned; they were sawed in two;
they were put to death by the sword....
HEBREWS 11:37 NIV

The prophet Zechariah was a prophet of restoration during the rebuilding of the temple in Jerusalem. One night the word of the Lord came to him. "I saw in the night, and behold, a man riding on a red horse! He was standing among the myrtle trees in the glen, and behind him were red, sorrel, and white horses" (Zechariah 1:8 ESV). An angel told him, "These are they whom the LORD has sent to patrol the earth" (Zechariah 1:10 ESV). Why should we be surprised? God sends His angels as emissaries over the whole earth to keep watch over us. It is important for us to remember that God knows everything. Zechariah exhorted the people to keep building the temple instead of giving in to discouragement. Yet when he called them to account for breaking God's commandments, the people did not want to hear God's truth and instead ended Zechariah's life (Matthew 23:35).

FAITH CHECK

Myrtle blossoms are fragrant when crushed. In a similar way, the death of Zechariah was a fragrant aroma to God. His faithful prophet was martyred for speaking God's truth. His people killed many of God's prophets and they crucified Jesus Christ, His only Son. Speaking God's truth may cost you your life, but keeping the truth from others will cost them eternal life in heaven.

Christians are not so
much in danger when
they are persecuted as
when they are admired.

–CHARLES SPURGEON

◈ 55 ◈
WEDDED MISS

He brought me to the banqueting house,
and His banner over me was love.
SONG OF SOLOMON 2:4 KJV

The guests are seated on white wooden chairs festooned with flowers and ribbons. The bride, on the arm of her father, walks down the aisle on an immaculate white runner strewn with white rose petals. A young couple hold hands under a breathtaking canopy of roses, lilies, and gardenias. They exchange solemn vows before a smiling preacher. Weddings are almost always wonderful, joyful, emotional, fun events. They're like family reunions within a marriage union. However, some weddings are not like that at all. Things can go wrong. A bride might have a fainting spell at the altar from all the excitement. A mischievous groomsman pats a "Help Me" sign on the groom's back. The groom inadvertently steps on the bride's train or veil and rips it. A kid puts a frog in the punch bowl. The wedding cake tips over and smashes to the floor. An outdoor wedding plays host to a torrential downpour.

Perfect ceremonies don't make perfect marriages, but God is perfect, and when He is at the center of your relationship, He will help you remember and appreciate that your spouse is perfect for you no matter what your wedding day was like.

FAITH CHECK

Some weddings are slow-motion train wrecks where everything goes as wrong as wrong can be. But even if everything goes wrong during the ceremony and reception, when the couple are right for each other and right with God, it's all right. The "I do's" were said and the couple was wed.

That wedding was so
emotional even the
cake was in tiers.

★

THE QUICK AND THE DROOPY

As a dog returns to its vomit,
so a fool repeats his foolishness.
PROVERBS 26:11 NLT

Some believers came to the Lord with a colorful background of sin, a past with enough misadventure and sauciness to fill volumes. They have said it all and done it all, or so they think. If you've lived a lifetime of sin, you will only get better at it as time goes by. The Bible says that evil grows and is constantly devising greater evils (Proverbs 6:14). The goal of Christians is to follow Jesus so closely that sin doesn't have a chance to tempt us away. Does that happen? Nope. Sin tempts all of us away at times. King David had his share of sins, but what set him apart was his amazing heart of repentance. When confronted with the truth, he didn't lie or try to justify himself before God. He owned up to all of his sins and asked forgiveness, which is a good example for us to follow (Psalm 51:1-2). We're usually like Quick Draw McGraw when we sin and Droopy Dog when it comes to repenting. The closer we follow Jesus, the less we will want to sin, and our sins will become downright boring. Still sins, of course, but less tempting to return to as time goes by.

FAITH CHECK

American Bishop Fulton J. Sheen once said, "Hearing nuns' confessions is like being stoned to death with popcorn." Let us hope and pray that the only sins we commit are as boring, and that our sins are no more. Has anyone on this earth ever followed Christ so perfectly that they ceased to sin? Not likely, but we can sure try. The comfort is in knowing that we have forgiveness.

Little sins are
pioneers of hell.

–JAMES HOWELL

★

SHADOW OF THE OWL

Whatever you do, do it all for the glory of God.
I CORINTHIANS 10:31 NIV

erod the Great was rotten to the core, and his grandson Herod Agrippa the First didn't fall far from the tree. Herod ordered the death of the apostle James by sword, and when he saw that it pleased the Jews, he had Peter arrested as well. The more people praised Herod, the more he ate it up. Jesus said this of prideful people, "Whoever exalts himself will be humbled, and he who humbles himself will be exalted (Luke 14:11 NKJV). The people of Tyre and Sidon called upon Herod to speak, and a flattered Herod showed up in royal robes of silver that reflected brightly off the morning sun. When they saw him the people shouted, "It is the voice of a god and not of a man!" (Acts 12:22 AMP). Herod did not correct them or give God the glory. Which is right about when he saw an owl, a bad tiding to a superstitious man. Herod should have been worried about God's response to his pride instead of a bird, because at that moment an angel of the Lord struck him down and he was eaten up by worms and died five days later. Herod was eaten up with pride long before the worms got to him.

FAITH CHECK

Sometimes evil seems to triumph over God's people, but those triumphs always turn to tragedy for those who oppose God. Herod thought to spread fear when he had John the Baptist beheaded, but he unwittingly spread the Good News. God revealed Herod's true character and gave him a taste of his future in a place where the fire is never quenched and the worm never dies (Mark 9:48).

On the back of Satan's neck
is a nail-scarred footprint.

—C. S. LEWIS

THE LAST STRAW

Know this, my beloved brothers:
let every person be quick to hear,
slow to speak, slow to anger.
JAMES 1:19 ESV

Ever have those days where you wake up just plain ornery? Tail up and stinger out? A steady stream of stress is typically the cause. But anxiety or exhaustion can send your irritability soaring as well. And sometimes when you're not feeling well, any old thing can send you over the tipping point. But none of the possible causes matter at that moment when steam is fixing to blow out of the top of your head! We would rather blame someone or something else for "provoking" our mood, but *our* mood is within *our* power to change. To remain irritable is self-indulgent. "Love is patient and kind; love does not envy or boast; it is not arrogant or rude. It does not insist on its own way; it is not irritable or resentful" (I Corinthians 13:4–5 ESV).

FAITH CHECK

The Bible says that God does not have a short fuse (Exodus 34:6). He gives us a lot of grace, even when we flaunt our sins in His face. Yet He waits patiently for us to recognize our sins and repent. But there is a point at which God will yank us by the collar when He has had enough. The next time you're tempted to squeeze the irritation trigger, pull the parachute cord instead. Take yourself out of the situation. Don't delay, pray. Tell the Lord what's eating at you and repent. Then go back and apologize. Ask forgiveness of those whose feelings you have hurt. Children especially need to hear that adults are sorry for losing their temper.

In times like these,
it helps to recall that
there have always been
times like these.

–PAUL HARVEY

59
MAMA TOLD ME

Many women have done excellently,
but you surpass them all.
PROVERBS 31:29 ESV

Southern mamas have a lingo all their own when it comes to correcting their kids. "If you fall out of that tree and break your legs don't come running to me!" "Just wait till your daddy comes home!" "You can get glad in the same britches you got mad in." If you dare to tell your mama you're bored, you can expect a long list of chores to occupy your day. And if you back talk your mama she'll tell you, "God don't like ugly," and there's no way to answer that without asking for more trouble. Sometimes a mere look from your mama was enough to send chill bumps up and down your spine. Many a child truly believes that mothers have an extra set of eyes in the back of their heads. When mama said, "If you don't stop that crying I'll give you something to cry about," you knew she meant business. And with grown kids, mamas get more creative about how they say things. For instance, "Are you sure you want to do that?" really means your name has been added to the prayer list at Sunday school.

FAITH CHECK

Remember when your mama would say, "Someday you'll thank me for this"? Well, here's to all the mothers who cared enough to correct us, to make us go back to the candy store and pay for the gumball we "borrowed," to respect our elders, to be kind and helpful to others, to pray and go to church on Sunday.

If at first you don't
succeed, do it the way
mama told you to.

★

◈ 60 ◈
PRAY-TECTION

This is the confidence we have in approaching God:
that if we ask anything according to His will, He hears us.
I JOHN 5:14 NIV

If someone walks in on you talking to God, they're going to think you're crazier than a sprayed roach. But that's okay. Prayer is the wonderful way believers communicate with God. We confess our sins, tell Him our secrets, air life's hurts and frustrations to Him, and present our requests to Him when we pray. We praise Him. We sing. We dance. And other times it's nice to just sit in the big silence that God makes when He's there with you in the room. God doesn't need our prayers to act on our behalf; He requires them. Scripture calls for us to pray for those who persecute us (Matthew 5:44), to pray in the Spirit on all occasions with all kinds of prayers and requests (Ephesians 6:18), to devote ourselves to prayer, being watchful and thankful (Colossians 4:2), and to pray continually (I Thessalonians 5:17). Jesus was always going off by Himself to find a solitary place to pray. We should follow His example. Prayer is our greatest weapon against the enemy.

FAITH CHECK

When we pray for ourselves and our family, friends, coworkers, neighbors, country, and our world, a calm confidence replaces the worry and anxiety in our hearts. The fear that grips you is replaced by faith when we pray. Jesus saves, heals, protects, and delivers! Prayer brings God's pray-tection. Prayer brings God's provision. Prayer brings God's peace.

God shapes the world by
prayer. The more praying there
is in the world the better the
world will be, the mightier
the forces against evil.

– MOTHER TERESA

61
SHALT NOTS

Thou shall have no other gods before Me.
EXODUS 20:3 KJV

When you're listening to the radio there are inevitably commercials, and at the end of some, a person who sounds like Alvin and the Chipmunks starts talking at hyper-speed. The details about that great car deal or the disturbing side effects of a particular medication whiz past so fast you have no idea what the person just said. There's a wise old saying that the devil is in the details. In cases like these it certainly holds true. If you don't take the time to read the fine print on a legal document, you might find yourself in a mess of trouble after you sign. Some folks lie like they breathe. Fast-talking scoundrels count on getting the details past your conscious mind and getting your signature on the dotted line. The devil fast-talked Adam and Eve into eating the forbidden fruit by casting doubt on God's "shalt nots," but Adam and Eve failed to consider the consequences. On that day their eyes were opened to sin and their physical bodies were exposed to the ravages of age, sickness, pain, and death.

FAITH CHECK

God is truth and He is incapable of speaking anything other than His own character. There's no fine print or fast talk in anything He tells us. So the next time you hear someone talking the tongue out of their shoe, share the gospel truth with them instead.

You contribute nothing to your salvation except the sin that made it necessary.

—JONATHAN EDWARDS

★

PEARL RIVER

Then the angel showed me the river
of the water of life, bright as crystal, flowing
from the throne of God and of the Lamb.
REVELATION 22:1 ESV

The Pearl River forms the boundary between Louisiana and Mississippi and was so named due to a prominent feature of the water. The bottom of the pearl river is covered with pearl shells, which gives the water a unique luminescence that captivates the eye. Swamps beyond the river bank teem with life, from alligators and snakes among the river cane, to black bears and ivory-billed woodpeckers. Golden flecks of sunlight decorate the ground with the lacy patterns of sycamore, cypress, oak, and tupelo leaves. Many people settled there, but the area was originally home to the Choctaw people, who were known for the baskets they made from river cane that grew along the banks. The tribe lost their land and sacred burial grounds to the Treaty of Dancing Rabbit Creek in 1830, but 178 years later, the land was returned to them, a bittersweet celebration. Fresh cane is pliable when green but tans into tightly knit baskets as it dries. If you have endured a bitter loss or setback, are you still pliable to God?

FAITH CHECK

The Pearl River still flows as it did from the beginning, though it holds many sorrows. God has a river in heaven that is bright as crystal, flowing from the throne of God and of the Lamb. The freshwater mussel shells give luster to the sparkling water of the Pearl River, but New Jerusalem has the glory of God as its light and the Lamb is its lamp (Revelation 21:23).

Earth has no sorrow that heaven cannot heal.

—THOMAS MOORE,
IRISH POET

THE WRITING ON THE WALL

It is better to take refuge in the LORD
than to trust in man. It is better to take refuge
in the LORD than to trust in princes.
PSALM 118:8-9 ESV

In elementary school certain teachers favored what they liked to call "chalkboard discipline." If a child misbehaved, the teacher would draw a chalk circle on a chalkboard and the child would be ordered to stick their nose in the middle of that circle. Not a bad punishment if you don't count the humiliation in front of the whole class and the embarrassment of a chalk-daubed nose afterwards. If the teacher was really mad at you, though, he or she might draw the circle a bit higher on the blackboard so you'd have to stand on your tippy-toes just to hit the mark with your nose. Unlike the chalkboard discipline or the time-outs that most of us experienced, many have suffered harsh and extreme physical and emotional punishment, so much so that it is difficult for them to trust others. That missing element of trust can interfere with faith as well. If your earthly father was harsh or unfair, you assume that your heavenly Father is as well. But not even the best earthly father can compare with our heavenly Father.

FAITH CHECK

*God is dependable, consistent, and completely trustworthy.
"Those who know your name put their trust in you, for you,
O LORD, have not forsaken those who seek you" (Psalm 9:10
ESV). We learn to trust God, prayer by answered prayer. Our
personal experience with Him reveals His character to us,
and His character is deserving of our complete trust.*

Faith is a reasoning trust, a trust which reckons thoughtfully and confidently upon the trustworthiness of God.

–JOHN R. STOTT

❖ 64 ❖
HELP ME!
I'M ON A FAMILY VACATION

You gave a wide place for my steps under me,
and my feet did not slip.
PSALM 18:36 ESV

Some of us have fond and not-so-fond memories of family vacations. Cram a family into a loaded station wagon aimed toward a distant beach or mountain destination and you can expect more than a few skirmishes along the way. Siblings always get on one another's nerves, but especially so when they are cooped up in a car for hours on end. Sometimes you wake up to your little brother's filthy sock dangling over your nose. Or everyone wants the same toy, or no one wants to watch the movie you want to see. Besides all that, it is a well-known fact that every family has a carsick child. Without warning, that one kid will lose their lunch. Though astute moms or dads may notice the subtle signs and attempt to deploy a sick bag, the bag will never connect with the carsick kid in time to prevent the disaster. For the remainder of the trip and for however many years you own the vehicle, the scent of sour tummy will perfume the interior. Talk about enduring memories.

FAITH CHECK

Traveling with kids is enough to make a parent lose their mind. But there are moments that make it all worth it: when your child holds a seashell to his ear and tells you he's talking to God, or when you see your kids sharing and taking care of one another. But most of all, when the kids are completely exhausted after a long day of vacation fun, and they're all fast asleep. Vacation gold.

Silence is golden.
Unless you have kids.
Then silence
is suspicious.

★

65

ISSUES THAT
REQUIRE TISSUES

In Him we live and move and have our being...
for we are indeed his offspring.
ACTS 17:28 ESV

"If it was a snake it would have bit you!" A man can stand at the open refrigerator door asking his wife where the butter is yet be staring right at it. Some people are better at finding things than others. What makes them better? They look in the places others don't think to look. When you've been through the wringer and feel like God has left you all alone, where do you look when you're trying to find Him? Most would begin their search by reading the Bible or sinking to their knees in prayer. Those are the obvious starting points. But there is fallacy at the root of your search if you believe that God truly left you at the point that you needed Him most. If you're looking for God, the good news is you don't have far to go. God never left you at all. In fact, He promised that He would never leave us or forsake us (Hebrews 13:5).

FAITH CHECK

Is God in the middle of my situation or circumstance? Is God in the middle of my personal storm? Is He with me in the middle of my addiction? With me in the midst of my life-changing diagnosis? With me in my grief? My lawsuit? My loneliness? My loss? There are people who see God as distant and detached from the affairs of humanity. However, if that were so, He would not desire to dwell in our hearts.

But the secret to joy
is to keep seeking God
where we doubt He is.

−ANN VOSKAMP

★

66
BUT GOD

What is impossible with man is possible with God.
LUKE 18:27 ESV

You've prayed, fasted, searched God's Word, asked your friends and your church to pray, but the thing you expected God to do does not happen. You've come to the end of your hope. Is it time to give up? To accept that the answer is no? Soon after the apostle James was beheaded, Peter was thrown into prison, bound in chains between two soldiers with sentries guarding him (Acts 12:6). His situation looked hopeless. Peter was probably thinking, "I guess I'm next." But God sent an angel that night and the heavy chains fell off his hands. The doors opened and Peter walked out. The minor prophet Habakkuk grew impatient waiting for an answer to his prayers, "How long, LORD, must I call for help, but You do not listen?" (Habakkuk 1:2 NIV). Your situation might look hopeless, beyond restoration, or completely past help. But God. When you are caught in the teeth of an impossible situation and there is no way out, God is your only plan. *Wait* without *worrying* and you *will* see the Lord *work* in His perfect timing (Hebrews 10:36).

FAITH CHECK

Seek the kingdom of God and His righteousness first (Matthew 6:33). Ask in prayer and believe that you have received it (Mark 11:24). Have faith, not fear (II Timothy 1:7). "Without faith it is impossible to please him, for whoever would draw near to God must believe that he exists and that he rewards those who seek him" (Hebrews 11:6 ESV).

If you are going to live by faith, then expect your faith to be tested. A faith that cannot be tested can't be trusted.

–WARREN W. WIERSBE

67

THE SCENT OF A STORM

He said to the crowd:
"When you see a cloud rising in the west,
immediately you say, 'It's going to rain,' and it does."
LUKE 12:54 NIV

Grandpas always seem to know when a storm is on its way before anyone else does. From a porch rocking chair the man could predict the weather by scent alone. And when the thunder started rattling the sky he'd tell you the tale of Rip Van Winkle and the old men bowling nine-pins. Have you ever tilted your nose up to catch a whiff of a storm and the first drops of rain? The scent is distinct, clean and crisp to the nose. The scent of ozone. The smell of spring rain on the soil. Green, earthy, and pungent. A heady fragrance of earth and sky. And electricity. Lightning heats the air to fifty thousand degrees when it strikes. The rapid expansion of air creates thunder, that scary sonic boom that sends your dog quivering under the nearest bed. When lightning heats the air, it splits the bonds between nitrogen and oxygen. Although most pair up again as the air cools, some odd pairings occur that produce ozone. A storm might be miles away but the gust at the front of a storm carries it ahead of the rain straight to your nose. Grandpa was right about his uncanny ability to smell a storm coming.

FAITH CHECK

Sometimes God gives us little signs that storms are coming in our lives, but other times storms seem to come up out of nowhere (Mark 4:37). The best way to prepare for a storm is to remain in a constant state of readiness. Build your life on a firm foundation. Cover yourself and your loved ones in prayer daily. And let the light of God guide you and keep you on the right path.

Faith is taking a step in
the same direction the
evidence is pointing.

—LEE STROBEL

68

BEST FRIENDS

A man of many companions may come to ruin,
but there is a friend who sticks closer than a brother.
PROVERBS 18:24 ESV

If you are blessed to have a best friend, you have a real treasure in your life. You have a person who knows you as well as you know them. Someone you can trust. Pray with. Cry with. Laugh with. A person you have true affection for. A friend you can always count on to help you when you need them most. A best friend who knows your secrets, has seen you in every state from Cloud Nine to a puddle of stagnant water, yet persists in loving and supporting you. But as wonderful as your best friend on earth is, he or she is not as good a friend as we have in Jesus. Sometimes a faithful friend will fail to help you in your time of need through no fault of their own. Or turn on you and betray your trust. Or pass away to glory ahead of you. The point is that no friend can ever be as good a friend as we have in Jesus because no friend can be the kind of friend that He is. Jesus will never fail you, never leave you, never forsake you (Hebrews 13:5), in your life here on earth and forever after. A dear friend is a blessing from God, but Jesus is the dearest friend of all.

FAITH CHECK

Jesus is loving and loyal, a faithful forever friend. He intercedes for us, defends us, sends His angels to protect us. Offers encouragement. Answers prayers. Comforts our hearts when they are breaking. Gives us peace in the midst of turmoil. Fills us with hope in hopeless situations. Sits with us when everyone else scatters. He loved us so much He gave His life on the cross for us.

The dearest friend on earth is a mere shadow compared to Jesus Christ.

–OSWALD CHAMBERS

QUALITY FRIENDSHIPS

Two friends enlisted in the military and were sent overseas. They fought alongside one another and during an enemy attack, one of the men was mortally wounded. Unable to crawl back to the foxhole, he lay dying, stuck in the middle of crossfire. The cries of his wounded friend spurred the other man to action. The sergeant warned him not to go, that it was too late to save his friend, but the man was determined to help him. He struggled to make his way back to the foxhole, his dead friend cradled in his arms. The sergeant, both angry and moved by what the man had done for his friend told him that what he'd done for his friend wasn't worth wasting his life too, that his friend was dead and now he too lay wounded and dying. The man gasped for breath and cried, "Oh yes, it was Sarge. When I got to him, the only thing he said was, 'I knew you'd come, Jim'."

SOURCE: ADAPTED FROM

https://www.amazon.com/Quality-Friendship-Gary-Inrig/
dp/0802428916 Gary Inrig, Quality Friendships, (Chicago, Moody Press, 1981), p. 71.

69
UNIQUELY YOU

He who began a good work in you
will bring it to completion at the day of Jesus Christ.
PHILIPPIANS 1:6 ESV

On the Lord's Day in church somebody's always singing the Sunday Special. And if you've sat in those pews enough over the years you know that ten people can sing the same song, but they won't sing it the same way. The person who was born with the right voice to sing a particular song will sing it to perfection. Sing it with their whole heart, sing with their very soul.

God created each of us for something special. We may spend half our lives piddling around doing all sorts of other things rather than answer the call of God to do the thing He called us to do. It's easy to talk ourselves out of doing what our hearts are nudging us towards. We convince ourselves that we can't, that we're not good enough, that its impossible for however many reasons. Has God called you to the missionary field? To write a book? To the ministry? To sing? Then do it. You might not be very good at it at first, but with God's help, you will be. Surrender your doubt, your fear, and your insecurities to God and answer the call to your life's work, whatever it may be. God can create an extraordinary work in your hands that would be an ordinary work in someone else's.

FAITH CHECK

The work God has called you to do will not produce the same results if somebody else does it. You are unique and special, created for a purpose and a reason, designed by our Creator to produce the maximum results from your gifts, talents, and willing heart. Others can sing the song, but nobody on this earth will sing it quite like you.

Your potential
is the sum of all the
possibilities God
has for your life.

—CHARLES STANLEY

70

THE FURNACE
OF AFFLICTION

I have refined you, but not as silver;
I have tested you in the furnace of affliction.
ISAIAH 48:10 NKJV

When you're in pain or grief, there is no rush to do anything. There are no important deadlines, no occasions or celebrations, no reasons to think about anything else. Food does not tempt you. Entertainment is an empty promise. You can't sleep. Sunny days only exist outside your darkened room. Suffering humbles and brings you to your knees. Your strengths and weaknesses begin to surface through the irritation of the physical or emotional wounds, and you see who you really are inside. God skims off the products of affliction, our weaknesses and faults that float to the top, and refines and purifies us to a greater extent through this process. When you have experienced pain, you develop a deep, heartfelt compassion for others who are suffering, and you comfort others more effectively than if you had never experienced pain. People who are hurting are more likely to trust and receive words of comfort from others who have gone through what they are going through. The fruits of affliction can minister in mighty ways. Your pain can offer gain to someone else in need of hope.

FAITH CHECK

You can be angry at God as long as you're honest with Him about what you're feeling, and as long as you keep up the conversation. He will comfort you and give you peace in your darkest hours.

Sanctified afflictions are spiritual promotions.

-MATTHEW HENRY

★

71

WORD DARTS

Thoughtless words can wound as deeply as any sword,
but wisely spoken words can heal.
PROVERBS 12:18 GNT

If you've been around long enough, you might remember a nostalgic game called Lawn Darts. The game involved a plastic target circle you would place on the lawn and a handful of weighted spikes you would toss in the air one by one with the hope of landing within the target area. What could go wrong? The trouble with this game was of course the weighted spikes. Sometimes they landed where they weren't supposed to, with devastating consequences.

God said that life and death are in the power of the tongue and those who love it will eat its fruits (Proverbs 18:21 ESV). Yet we randomly throw out words every day like lawn darts without a thought as to where or how they will land. Words can hurt others deeply or heal like a comforting balm. Given the choice, wouldn't you rather speak words of healing and comfort to others? Word darts are as reckless, dangerous, and unpredictable as lawn darts.

FAITH CHECK

Your words can have a negative or positive effect on you as well. For instance, if you are praying and confessing God's Word over a situation in your life yet out of the other side of your mouth you're confessing failure, you are sabotaging the very outcome you're praying for! There are definitely instances where using a glue stick instead of Chapstick on our lips would be more helpful!

Words are seeds that
do more than blow
around. They land in our
hearts, not the ground.

— UNKNOWN

★

POEM:
MY BIBLE

Pages frail, this tattered text
covered me as I travailed, and
watermarked them with my tears,
through days, turned into years;

My every question seemed to be,
"Why, Lord, Why"?
I found each answer written there,
in love, especially for me;

Oh, I consumed them one by one,
by chapter and by verse,
I knew each page by touch,
In forward and reverse;

But something happened,
subtly first, a busy life intruded,
my hungry soul a wasted frame,
no daily bread renewed it;

My life, my love, my peace, my rest,
Once clutched tightly to my breast,
Now shut, now shrouded, silent dust,
Words of life I used to trust,

I reached, I grasped at binding loosed,
by years of time and frequent use,
Crackled leather, ancient balm,
Filled my troubled heart with calm,

My Faithful Friend still welcomed me,
As if I were not gone at all,
I smiled and settled in my chair,
To read about the prodigal.

By Linda P. Kozar, 2003

SWORD OF THE SPIRIT

*All Scripture is breathed out by God and profitable
for teaching, for reproof, for correction, and for training
in righteousness, that the man of God may be complete,
equipped for every good work.*
II TIMOTHY 3:16–17 ESV

Back in the day, lots of people carried handy-dandy pocketknives with them wherever they went, not for violent intent but for utilitarian purposes. The first version was called a soldier's knife, and equipped military personnel with practical survival tools like a foldable knife, can opener, screwdriver, and more. But the most useful pocketknife to carry around was undoubtedly the Swiss Army knife. The handy gadget originally contained various blades, nail file/cleaner, wood saw, scissors, pliers, bottle opener, tweezers, corkscrew, screw driver, etc. Modern versions contain extras like an electrician's blade, pruning blade, bit driver, LED light, USB stick, magnifying lens, awl, pen, ruler, nail-fillers, counter sinkers, reamer, hook, chisel, and toothpick. A multi-tool gadget might transform an ordinary person into an instant "McGyver," ready to fend off an alligator or hot-wire a rocket. But a Swiss Army knife is mostly handy when you need to cut cardboard boxes or snip a loose thread off a shirt. Tools are only useful if you actually use them.

FAITH CHECK

The Bible is better than a Swiss Army knife, but only if you use it. Like a sword, the Bible pierces "to the division of soul and spirit…discerning the thoughts and intentions of the heart" (Hebrews 4:12 ESV). God's Word saves, heals, protects, and delivers. His Word can demolish strongholds, defend the gospel to others, take every thought captive (II Corinthians 10:4–5), and so much more.

God's Word is a believer's
Swiss Army knife for
every situation.

—LINDA KOZAR

★

AN ATTITUDE OF GRATITUDE

Let the peace of Christ rule in your hearts,
since as members of one body you were called to peace.
And be thankful.
COLOSSIANS 3:15 NIV

When you did something good as a child you got a nice pat on your head, and if you were really, really good, you scored a hair tousle with an "Atta boy!" or an "Atta girl!" And you delighted in that approval. Those pats on the head are something we miss as adults. Approval and positive reinforcement seem to be reserved only for children. But even a mosquito gets a pat on the back when he's doing his job. What if we extended that kindness and grace throughout life?

FAITH CHECK

Try offering genuine compliments to your spouse, thanking them for all they do at home, at work, and with the kids. Thank your grandparents for the sacrifices they made for the family over the years. Show your appreciation to your parents for raising, supporting, and loving you. Maybe they paid for your education or helped you buy your first car. Thank them. Offer gratitude to your neighbors for keeping an eye on your house whenever you're away. Tell them that simple act of kindness means so much to you. Thank the UPS delivery person who delivers packages to your home. And the mail delivery person. Thank the person who cuts and styles your hair. And the woman who does your nails. Thank your doctor and your dentist. Thank your pastor for preaching a good sermon. Most of all, be thankful to God, who forgives you and calls you His own, your Daddy God who hugs your soul when you make Him proud. His approval means everything.

And when I give thanks
for the seemingly
microscopic, I make
a place for God to
grow within me.

—ANN VOSKAMP

★

LOVE'S END ZONE

My command is this:
Love each other as I have loved you.
JOHN 15:12 NIV

The first time you hold your newborn baby in your arms and gaze at that amazing little face, it is hard to imagine loving any child more. As your family expands, you wonder whether you'll be able to love your new baby as much as you love your first. But you do. And your heart overflows with love for your children.

The more we surrender our hearts to loving others, the more God expands our capacity to love. Love does not have a natural end zone. God has given us an ever-expanding ability to love. The more you choose to love others, the more you will be able to love. "Whoever does not love does not know God, because God is love" (I John 4:8 NIV). Love is not easy. Sometimes it seems downright impossible to love certain people in your life, especially those who hurt your heart, but when you pray for and forgive them, God heals your hurt and transforms your heart so you are able to love those who hate you and bless those who curse you.

FAITH CHECK

When you plant love, in time you will reap its harvest. Do you have the bandwidth to handle so much affection? You do indeed! The Bible compares growth and expansion to tent pegs. If you pound your tent pegs into the ground a few feet farther apart, the tent will stretch to accommodate that extra room. "Make your tents large. Spread out! Think big! Use plenty of rope, drive the tent pegs deep" (Isaiah 54:2 THE MESSAGE). So it is with the human heart. Love more and you will have more room in your heart to love.

Lord, grant that I might
not so much seek to
be loved as to love.

-FRANCIS OF ASSISI

◆ 75 ◆
THE CARE WE GIVE

Come to Me, all you who labor and are heavy laden,
and I will give you rest.
MATTHEW 11:28 NKJV

Caregiving is one of the toughest jobs any of us can ever be called on to do. Taking care of an elderly parent is especially hard. When the parent/child roles reverse we are tasked with changing our whole way of life in order take on a challenging and difficult work. The sudden loss of personal freedom is the first thing most caregivers miss. Becoming a shut-in with the shut-in you are caring for is tough too. And attending to intimate bodily functions is a task definitely not for the faint of heart, even if *you* are. Caregivers do what they have to do. They dispense medications and attend to wounds, perform housekeeping duties, laundry, and meal prep, take trips to the doctor's office and hospital, and more. The mental challenges are rough as well. An Alzheimer's or dementia patient will ask the same question a thousand times a day. The stress and strain are overwhelming. But the worst day of all is the day your parent no longer knows who you are.

FAITH CHECK

Caregivers must manage their expectations. We cannot expect an elderly parent to behave like they used to. The dull eyes that stare straight ahead used to light up when you entered the room. The loving arms that once embraced you do not stir. The body has a tenuous hold on life, but there is an eternal soul inside waiting to fly away to God's heavenly country. The face you love you will see again in due time and your loved one will rejoice to see you. Until then, care, give, love.

You have been assigned
this mountain to show
others it can be moved.

–MEL ROBBINS

BETTER HOMES AND GARDENS

Then the Lord God took the man and
put him in the garden of Eden to tend and keep it.
GENESIS 2:15 NKJV

If you grow your own vegetable garden or cultivate a good-sized kitchen garden, you know what a sun-drenched, vine-ripened, shiny red tomato smells like. The second your nose gets anywhere near the plant, that fragrant scent captivates you. Sweet and grassy, with a certain tang like the fuzz on the tendrils and vines, tomatoes hold a slightly herbal aroma, like the scent of rosemary and sultry summer sun. Poets write odes to them, and others write silly limericks. John Denver wrote a song about homegrown tomatoes. Of course, not everyone appreciates a tasty tomato, but Southerners sure like their 'mater sandwiches, fried green tomatoes, and chowchow, which if you aren't familiar is a tangy relish made from pickled green tomatoes. And let's not forget Southern tomato pie.

FAITH CHECK

It's easy to take the simple things in life for granted, but God obviously put a lot of thought into creating the tomato and we should appreciate and give thanks to God for everything. The next time you take a bite out of a tasty tomato sprinkled with sea salt, be sure to thank God. After all, without tomatoes we wouldn't have pizza!

It's difficult to think anything but pleasant thoughts while eating a homegrown tomato.

—LEWIS GRIZZARD

RECIPE:
SOUTHERN TOMATO PIE

INGREDIENTS:

PIECRUST *(Or buy a frozen crust and prepare according to directions).*
- 1-1/4 cups all-purpose flour
- 1/4 cup cold vegetable shortening, cut into pieces
- 4 tablespoons cold unsalted butter, cut into pieces
- 1/2 teaspoon sea salt (use fine)
- 3 to 4 Tbsp. ice-cold water

FILLING
- 2-1/4 pounds assorted tomatoes sliced thin (heirloom tomatoes are best)
- 1-1/4 teaspoons coarse sea salt, divided
- 1 sweet onion, chopped
- 1 1/4 teaspoons freshly ground pepper, divided
- 1 tablespoon canola oil
- 1/2 cup assorted chopped fresh herbs (such as chives, parsley, and basil)
- 1/2 cup freshly grated Gruyere cheese
- 1/2 cup freshly grated Parmigiano-Reggiano cheese
- 1/4 cup mayonnaise

DIRECTIONS:

PREPARE PIECRUST: Process flour, shortening, butter, and salt in food processor until mixture resembles coarse meal. With processor running, gradually add 3 Tbsp. ice-cold water, 1 Tbsp. at a time, and process until dough forms a ball and leaves sides of bowl, adding up to 1 Tbsp. more water, if necessary. Shape dough into a disk, and wrap in plastic wrap. Chill 30 minutes. Unwrap dough, and place on a lightly floured surface; sprinkle lightly with flour. Roll dough to 1/8-inch thickness. Preheat oven to 425°. Press dough into a 9-inch pie plate. Chill 30 minutes or until firm. Line piecrust with aluminum foil; fill with pie weights or dried beans to keep dough from bubbling. Place on an aluminum foil-lined baking sheet and bake at 425° for 20 minutes. Remove weights and foil. Bake 5 minutes or until browned. Cool completely on baking sheet on a wire rack (about 30 minutes). Reduce oven temperature to 350°.

PREPARE FILLING: Place tomatoes in a single layer on paper towels; sprinkle with 1 tsp. salt. Let stand 10 minutes. Meanwhile, sauté onion and 1/4 tsp. each salt and pepper in hot oil in a skillet over medium heat 3 minutes or until onion is tender. Pat tomatoes dry with a paper towel. Layer tomatoes, onion, and herbs in prepared crust, seasoning each layer with pepper (1 tsp. total). Stir together cheeses and mayonnaise; spread over pie. Bake at 350° for 30 minutes or until lightly browned. Shield edges with foil to prevent browning. Serve warm, or at room temperature.

SOURCE: ADAPTED FROM

https://www.myrecipes.com/recipe/old-fashioned-tomato-pie

GOD'S WAITING ROOM

*We know that in all things God works
for the good of those who love Him,
who have been called according to His purpose.*
ROMANS 8:28 NIV

American author E. M. Bounds (1835–1913), who wrote extensively on the subject of prayer, wrote about the reason Christians fail so often to get answers to their prayers. "They just drop down and say a few words, and then jump up and forget it and expect God to answer them. Such praying always reminds me of the small boy ringing his neighbor's door bell and then running away as fast as he can go." What E. M. Bounds said back then still "rings" true, especially in this day and age when we want everything and we want it now. If your prayers aren't being answered maybe you ought to consider what kind of prayers you are praying. Did you ask God to smite an aggravating coworker? Reality check. God is not your hitman. If you think He is then you have no idea who *He* really is. Is your heart right with God? Though we think we're waiting on God, He's more than likely waiting on us to get right with Him. Is there unforgiveness in your life? When there's hatred in your heart, there's no room for the blood of Jesus. Did you get frustrated and give up? His timing is perfect.

FAITH CHECK

It is okay to ask God what is holding things up. Ask Him to show you and He will. Keep praying. Keep waiting. And keep on trusting God until you receive your answer.

The day you plant the
seed is not the day
you eat the fruit.

★

BONES OF CONTENTION

Nothing is covered up that will not be revealed,
or hidden that will not be known.
LUKE 12:2 ESV

Every family has a skeleton or two in their closet. A hidden history or undisclosed piece of information that would cause shame, scandal, embarrassment, or even imprisonment in some cases. The expression compares trying to hide a family or personal secret to attempting to keep a dead body in a closet. Which brings us to Benjamin Franklin. In 1998, excavations in the basement of Benjamin Franklin's London home turned up over 1,200 bones, enough to piece together the skeletons of more than a dozen bodies. People wondered if a founding father of American could be a serial killer. Thankfully, a quick study of the history of the home revealed that Franklin's young friend and protégé William Hewson ran an anatomy lab and school in the house, which was a shady, unethical practice that involved grave robbing but was a way to gain useful knowledge of human anatomy at the time.

FAITH CHECK

We all do our best to keep the lid on family secrets, but as hard as we try to keep the ugly truth from coming out, God never fails to shine a spotlight on the very secret we are trying so desperately to conceal. Whether your family secrets are in the closet or the basement, there are no secrets from God, who knows everything about you. "Wouldn't God find out, since He knows the secrets in our hearts?" (Psalm 44:21 GW).

They went into my closets
looking for skeletons, but
thank God all they found
were shoes, beautiful shoes.

—IMELDA MARCOS

79
FAMILY MATTERS

Avoid foolish controversies, genealogies,
dissentions, and quarrels about the law,
for they are unprofitable and worthless.
TITUS 3:9 ESV

ots of people are interested in having their DNA tested these days. They're interested in finding out more about their ancestors and what their family tree looks like. Some families keep detailed genealogy books that pass down from many generations back. They belong to exclusive societies, some dating back to relatives who came to America on the *Mayflower*. Others discover to their delight that they are related to royalty, aristocrats, or famous historical figures. We all want to feel important and special in some way. Researching ancestry sometimes provides us a reason to puff out our chests a bit in pride. Why should we care, though? The only life any of us has to live is the one we're living right now. The choices we make, the things we do on this earth, are the inspirations or warnings we leave to our descendants. There are many names written in the history of the world, but if those names are not written in God's Book of Life, they and the books their names are written in will turn to dust.

FAITH CHECK

Though we have many branches on our family tree, we all share the same root. We cannot choose who we are related to, but we can choose to serve God and be a blessing to others in this world, and offer the lasting legacy of a clean heart, a bowed knee, and a life lived by the book.

Every family tree
has a sap.

–DR. CHARLES LOWERY

★

THE FOUR GARDENS

Our citizenship is in heaven. And we eagerly await
a Savior from there, the Lord Jesus Christ.
PHILIPPIANS 3:20 NIV

sk anyone if they've ever read about a garden in the Bible and they'll say the Garden of Eden, of course, the garden where Adam and Eve sinned against God and were cast out. Some people will also remember reading about another garden, the Garden of Gethsemane, the garden of suffering where Jesus agonized at the separation from His Father that He would soon feel at the cross. Gethsemane means "olive press," appropriate because the weight of the world and all its sins would soon be put upon Him. But there are actually four gardens in the Bible. The site of Golgotha where Jesus was crucified was also known as the Garden of Golgotha, the site of the Garden Tomb where the body of Jesus was buried and resurrected on the third day. And the fourth garden is the Paradise of God (Revelation 2:7). Paradise means "Garden of Delight" and is the eternal garden where the tree of life grows and where believers will walk with God throughout all eternity.

FAITH CHECK

God walked with Adam and Eve in the Garden of Eden in the cool of the evening. Jesus likely walked with His disciples in the beautiful Garden of Gethsemane. Jesus walked alone to the cross at Golgotha to save mankind. And we will walk with God in His eternal garden in the New Jerusalem. No evil or temptation or sin will be allowed to enter the eternal garden of God, "but only those whose names are written in the Lamb's book of life" (Revelation 21:27 NIV).

Everything that God does
begins with a seed and
ends with a harvest.

★

ADORN YOUR HEART

*Do you not know that your body is a temple
of the Holy Spirit within you, whom you have from God?
You are not your own, for you were bought with a price.
So glorify God in your body.*
I CORINTHIANS 6:19-20 ESV

Grandmas have their own fashion aesthetic: colorful housecoats, knee-high hose rolled down to the ankles, and comfortable "tennie-runners" on their feet. Some people can't afford nice clothes so they wear what is given to them by charitable organizations or what they can afford to buy in resale shops. Some are dapper dressers who opt for the latest in chic and pay a hefty price tag for their fashion. Others dress like they are perpetual campers. And some folks aim for maximum comfort, dressing in the same "play clothes" every day, consisting of T-shirts and sports shorts. Look around you, though, and you will see lots of people in various stages of *undress*. Sure, Adam and Eve didn't wear any clothes, but to be fair, they didn't know they were naked until sin took up residence in the world. For believers, modesty isn't so much about covering up, it's about revealing your dignity. Most of us are overly preoccupied with how we dress. We constantly buy work clothes, play clothes, church clothes, vacation clothing, evening wear, maternity clothes, swimwear and holiday wear. Face it, our closets are never full enough.

FAITH CHECK

God is not impressed by expensive designer clothes, nor is He put off by old or dirty garments. He cares about the person inside the garment. When you open your heart to Him, He clothes you in His righteousness (Zechariah 3:4) and wraps His love around you.

Sometimes ready-to-wear is ready-to-error but God loves us no matter what we wear.

RIGHTEOUS LOT

*The two angels came to Sodom in the evening,
and Lot was sitting in the gate of Sodom.
When Lot saw them, he rose to meet them
and bowed himself with his face to the earth.*

GENESIS 19:1 ESV

braham's nephew Lot chose to live in the city of Sodom. He was greatly grieved by the depravity surrounding him and likely tried to help strangers and visitors whenever he could (II Peter 2:8). However, Lot's life was so full of compromise that not another soul in the city, including his family, had been influenced by his testimony. The two angels did not show up at the city gates flapping their wings; they appeared as ordinary men. Lot knew he had to protect them and he tried, but the men of the city surrounded his house and demanded that he bring the two strangers out to them. Sexual violence was normal, accepted behavior in Sodom. The angels pulled Lot back inside, shut the door, and struck the men who were at the doorway with blindness (Genesis 19:10–11). The people of Sodom were already blind spiritually. Now they could not see their way to sin.

FAITH CHECK

Today every believer sits at the gate of this world mourning the continuous evil they see and hear. While we cannot separate ourselves from the world we live in, we can sanctify our lives to God by living according to His Word and standing against evil. We can intercede, pray God's Word, and ultimately prevail against all the works of the enemy and speak words of life to others. God has planted each of us where we are for a reason. Find your gate and take your place.

A dog barks when his master is attacked. I would be a coward if I saw that God's truth is attacked and yet would remain silent.

–JOHN CALVIN

THE BLOOD NEVER LIES

In Him we have redemption through His blood,
the forgiveness of sins, in accordance
with the riches of God's grace.
EPHESIANS 1:7 NIV

Doctors say that the blood never lies. No matter how a patient spins their story of living a healthy lifestyle, lab test results will reveal how they live their life, what they eat and drink, and much more. Did you know that each person has a biological and a chronological age? You may be sixty chronologically but your blood identifies you biologically as someone ten years younger. The levels in a small group of proteins in your blood will reveal if you are at a greater risk to develop Alzheimer's disease. A blood test can reveal if you've suffered a concussion, whether you're dehydrated or clinically depressed, and will identify antibodies from the viruses you've recovered from. A simple blood test can reveal if you are prone to alcoholism, or if you suffer from anxiety. Your body releases specific proteins when you are distressed or agitated, and those levels will distinguish normal levels of anxiety from levels that are more concerning. No matter how diligent we are about maintaining our health, our bodies will eventually give out and we will pass from here to the hereafter. But the blood of Jesus tells an eternal story in us.

FAITH CHECK

Our debts are paid (Ephesians 1:7), and we are justified, forgiven, and declared righteous, cleansed, protected (Exodus 12:13), spared from the wrath of God, free (Galatians 3:13), healed (Isaiah 53:5), and holy. We have fellowship with God through His blood (Hebrews 10:19), and He has given us authority over the devil through the blood of Christ (Revelation 12:11).

Jesus took the tree
of death so you could
have the tree of life.

-TIM KELLER

84

THE STARRY CLUSTER

Christ also suffered once for sins, the just for the unjust,
that He might bring us to God, being put to death
in the flesh but made alive by the Spirit.
I PETER 3:18 NKJV

As a child, Amy Carmichael desperately wanted blue eyes instead of brown. She prayed but was disappointed that her eyes remained brown. She was passionate about sharing Christ but suffered from neuralgia, a condition that often left her bedridden for weeks or months at a time. She began a ministry to the "Shawlies," young Irish women who were so poor they could not afford hats to attend church, later ministering to the "mill girls of Manchester" in England. After that, Amy felt called to Japan as a missionary before going to India in 1901, where she accomplished most of her missionary work. Amy disguised herself as a local in order to visit the temples where she witnessed many "temple children," both girls and boys who were given over to prostitution by their parents to earn money. Over the years, Amy was able to rescue more than one thousand children from sex trafficking, though she risked prison to do so. She said, "When I consider the cross of Christ, how can anything I do be called sacrifice?"

FAITH CHECK

Amy Carmichael was thankful for her brown eyes because she resembled the people who were dear to her heart. She lived and worked with a group of persecuted Indian believers, women who were called "the Starry Cluster." They set up an orphanage, a hospital, and more to help rescued children attain a blessed future. India outlawed temple prostitution in 1948.

All that grieves is but for a moment. All that pleases is but for a moment. Only the eternal is important.

–AMY CARMICHAEL

HOW MANY STARS?

How many stars are visible in the night sky? There are 9,096 stars that are potentially visible across the entire sky. However, depending on conditions and seasons, and the hemisphere you are one, only half (4,548) stars are visible in a dark sky.

Our galaxy, the Milky Way is home to 100 billion stars but there are 10 billion galaxies in the observable universe. And if there are about 100 billion stars in each of those galaxies, there could be a whopping one billion trillion stars in the observable universe. This amount is about equal to the number of grains of sand on all the beaches of the earth. God told Abraham, "I will surely bless you, and I will surely multiply your offspring as the stars of heaven and as the sand that is on the seashore. And your offspring shall possess the gate of his enemies (Genesis 22:17 ESV).

SOURCE:

https://www.skyandtelescope.com/astronomy-resources/how-many-stars-night-sky-09172014/

https://scienceline.ucsb.edu/getkey.php?key=3775

85

GOD OF THE IMPOSSIBLE

Believe in the Lord Jesus Christ,
and you will be saved—you and your household.
ACTS 16:31 NIV

Severely beaten with rods and shackled in an inner cell of a heavily guarded prison, Paul and Silas were also fastened into painful foot stocks for good measure. Regardless of whatever fate that awaited them, though, Paul and Silas sang hymns to glorify God's name instead of giving in to pain or fear or despair. Suddenly, a violent earthquake struck and the foundations of the prison were shaken. Their chains fell off. However, the two noticed that the jailer was about to fall on his sword, the fate of all guards who allowed prisoners to escape. Instead of running, they assured the jailer that all the prisoners would stay put. The man in charge of the prison was himself a prisoner of darkness, but he was set free that night. The jailer and his whole family gave their lives to the Lord. Paul and Silas cared more about saving souls than saving their own lives.

FAITH CHECK

The famed magician and illusionist Harry Houdini used to up the ante with his magic stunts to make it seem as if there was no possible way he could work his way out of handcuffs, chains, and a straitjacket while upside-down in a tank of cold water. But he performed his acts by way of cleverly planned and rehearsed tactics. Our God is the real deal, and when the odds are stacked against us He loves to rescue us in great ways from impossible situations and show us that all things are possible for those who believe (Mark 9:23).

When you enter
His presence with praise,
He enters your
circumstances with power.

★

FOLLOW THE TRUE LEADER

*Love the L*ORD *your God and keep His requirements,*
His decrees, His laws and His commands always.
DEUTERONOMY 11:1 NIV

There are those who view the early church as little more than "primitive Christians" who saw the world in a myopic way, not a grand modern vision of progressive morality and cultural tempo. They call into question the Ten Commandments, the Great Commission (Matthew 28:18–20), the Lord's Supper (I Corinthians 11:26), God's stance on divorce, the definition of life, and much more. Every command of God, every Scripture, and every historical account is brought into question and up for debate. Some envision a recalibrated, modern update of the Bible, a set of rules they would be comfortable following, and have rewritten their versions of God's Word to suit societal sensibilities. However, Christianity cannot be edited or modernized to suit our taste or lifestyle, likes or dislikes. God's Word is not supposed to be easy to obey or convenient or comfortable but is meant to convict us of sin and to guide us to a holy, sanctified life with Christ.

FAITH CHECK

Culture does not define Christianity. Believers are Christ-followers, not culture-followers. God's Word is not evolutionary. His Word is revolutionary. The Bible goes against the grain of modern ideas of right and wrong, sin and morality. God's Word rubs some people the wrong way and brings others to repentance and right standing with Him. Where do you stand?

Biblical hope is not wishful thinking or an optimistic outlook; rather it is a confident expectation based on the certainty of God's Word that as He has anchored us in the past, so He will in the future.

—DAVID WILKERSON

SPEAK TO YOUR MOUNTAIN!

You will say to this mountain, "Move from here to there,"
and it will move; and nothing will be impossible for you.
MATTHEW 17:20 NKJV

Have you ever pointed to a mountain in your life and cried out to God in fear and desperation? *Do You see what I'm up against, Lord? Can't You see what's in front of me?* Of course He does. But God has already equipped us with a faith weapon to obliterate that blockage or obstruction in your life. And the ammunition, believe it or not, is no bigger than a mustard seed. If you've never seen a mustard seed, it is basically a teeny-tiny dot. Jesus is informing us that if the only faith we have in our arsenal is as teeny-tiny as a mustard seed, we can command mountains to move out of our way! Now imagine if you had a whole lot more faith in your arsenal than that one tiny seed. Like a whole jar of mustard seeds. Think about what we could do for the kingdom of God, especially if we joined our faith together in prayer.

FAITH CHECK

Command that mountain of sickness or disease to move in Jesus's name! "Heal me, O LORD, and I will be healed" (Jeremiah 17:4 NIV). Tell that mountain of anxiety to go in Jesus's name! "Do not let your hearts be troubled and do not be afraid" (John 14:27 NIV). Hurl those financial problems far away! "My God will meet all your needs according to the riches of His glory in Christ Jesus" (Philippians 4:19 NIV). Toss that mountain of unforgiveness into the sea in Jesus's name! "As the Lord has forgiven you, so you also must forgive" (Colossians 3:13 ESV). Speak to your mountain!

I have a mustard seed
and I'm not afraid
to use it.

88

FIREPROOF

If you declare with your mouth, "Jesus is Lord,"
and believe in your heart that God raised Him
from the dead, you will be saved.
ROMANS 10:9 NIV

Covered in sores, the poor man Lazarus sat at a rich man's gate to beg for scraps. In time Lazarus and the rich man both died. From the agony of hell's fire, the rich man looked up and saw Lazarus with Abraham and begged him to send Lazarus back from the dead to warn his five brothers to repent. However, Abraham told the man, "If they do not listen to Moses and the Prophets, they will not be convinced even if someone rises from the dead" (Luke 16:31 NIV). People put up a lot of excuses to avoid committing their life to Christ. "I'm not ready yet; I'm having too much fun," or, "I don't think I can give up all the things you have to give up to be a Christian." Others say, "I believe we all go to heaven when we die. I wouldn't want to serve a God who would be so cruel as to send people to hell forever." Jesus rose from the dead and yet some refuse to believe the *He is* the Resurrection and the Life. God is not cruel. He loves us so much He sent His only Son, who is without sin, to pay for our sins (John 3:16).

FAITH CHECK

The rich man's name is not mentioned. Perhaps riches and wealth and the fire of worldly desires were his true identity. Lazarus lived a life of misery and want yet held the priceless wonder of the eternal promise in his heart. The greatest treasure we could ever want is completely free of charge yet few are willing to receive it.

O unbeliever, you said,
"I cannot believe,"
but it would be more
honest if you had said,
"I will not believe." Your
unbelief is your fault,
not your misfortune.

—CHARLES SPURGEON

★

89

THE BRONZE SERPENT

*The LORD sent fiery serpents among the people
and they bit the people, so that many people of Israel died.*
NUMBERS 21:6 NASB

God called Moses to craft a bronze or copper rendition of a serpent and attach it to a pole in order to save the Israelites from dying from the deadly bites of fiery serpents He had sent to punish them for speaking against God and Moses (Numbers 21:4–9). The snakebites were deadly with a slower-acting, painful venom that would take days to claim a victim—long enough, however, for the victim to decide to obey God and look at the pole or die in stubborn rebellion. God had promised Moses that anyone who was bitten and looked to the bronze serpent would live. Believe it or not, some of the Israelites decided to worship the bronze serpent for many years afterwards. King Hezekiah, in enacting religious reform, tore down the pagan altars, cut down symbols of Asherah, and destroyed the "Nehustan," a derogatory term meaning "thing of brass," that he is said to have coined for the pagan version of the snake on a stick.

FAITH CHECK

The Bronze Serpent serves as a foreshadowing of Jesus's death on the cross. "As Moses lifted up the serpent in the wilderness, even so must the Son of man be lifted up (John 3:14 NKJV). "As the brass serpent had the appearance of a serpent and yet lacked its venom...He [Jesus] would have the appearance of a sinner, and yet be without sin" (Fulton J. Sheen).

The Jews looked upon a serpent to be freed from serpents; and we look upon the death of Christ to be delivered from death.

—ST. AUGUSTINE

90

THE GIFT OF NICODEMUS

Unless one is born of water and the Spirit,
he cannot enter the kingdom of God.

JOHN 3:5 NKJV

Scholar, Pharisee, and member of the Sanhedrin, Nicodemus was a man who knew the law inside and out. He decided to judge for himself who Jesus was. To protect his reputation, he visited the "Light of the world" under cover of darkness. Nicodemus didn't understand at first what Jesus meant by being "born again." He knew the law but he didn't know grace until he met Jesus. After Calvary, Nicodemus gathered an opulent offering of one hundred pounds of myrrh and sweet Indian aloes, worth a lifetime of wages, to anoint the body of Jesus. Was his gift to celebrate a royal burial for the Son of God or to celebrate Jesus's resurrection? Nicodemus brought his extravagant gift in the light of day as a disciple, no longer a seeker. Lazarus's sister Mary anointed the feet of Jesus for His burial with a pound of fragrance that filled a house, but the gift of Nicodemus filled the city with the fragrant announcement of resurrection and redemption for all.

FAITH CHECK

Nicodemus gave everything he had to Jesus: his fortune, his career, and his heart. There is a cost in this world to following Jesus (Matthew 16:24). Nicodemus found what he could not find in the law: abounding grace bought with the blood of Jesus. Whatever we lose or give up in this temporary life is nothing to what we will gain in our eternal life with Christ.

All your robes are
fragrant with myrrh
and aloes and cassia.

PSALM 45:8 NIV

LIVE YOUR FAITH

Dear Friend,

This book was prayerfully crafted with you, the reader, in mind—every word, every sentence, every page—was thoughtfully written, designed, and packaged to encourage you...right where you are this very moment. At DaySpring, our vision is to see every person experience the life-changing message of God's love. So, as we worked through rough drafts, design changes, edits and details, we prayed for you to deeply experience His unfailing love, indescribable peace, and pure joy. It is our sincere hope that through these Truth-filled pages your heart will be blessed, knowing that God cares about you—your desires and disappointments, your challenges and dreams.

He knows. He cares. He loves you unconditionally.

BLESSINGS!
THE DAYSPRING BOOK TEAM

Additional copies of this book and
other DaySpring titles can be purchased
at fine bookstores everywhere.
Order online at dayspring.com
or
by phone at 1-877-751-4347